1 KINGS
FROM START2FINISH

MICHAEL WHITWORTH

ISBN 978-1-941972-41-0

Published by Start2Finish
Bend, Oregon 97702
start2finish.org

Printed in the United States of America

Cover Design: Evangela Creative

CONTENTS

1

SOLOMON BECOMES KING

1 KINGS 1-2

Objective: To discover how God
accomplishes his will in uncertain times

INTRODUCTION

The opening narrative of 1 Kings is ripe with all the things we try to keep
away from children: sleazy back-room politics, royal family intrigue,
threats of murder and assassination, and a national beauty pageant, the
winner of which gets to sleep in the old king's bed. However, we must bear
in mind that the divine narrator approvingly relates these events to establish Solomon as the wise and legitimate heir to David's throne.

EXAMINATION

Read 1 Kings 1. David was about seventy years old and lay dying. His aides
brought him a young, attractive woman. Though they did so under the
guise of trying to warm David, his aides' true agenda is exposed with the
note that David "had no sexual relations with her" (v. 4 NIV). Bizarre as it
may sound to us, if David couldn't "conquer" the beautiful young Abishag
in the bedroom, the king was considered by some to be unfit to rule. Thus,

David's son, Adonijah, began plotting to replace his father.

It was almost unprecedented for anyone but the oldest surviving son to inherit the throne. Adonijah was indeed David's oldest surviving son, and no other precedent existed in Israel. Adonijah may have only been doing what was expected. But what kind of son seizes political power while his father is still alive? The narrator may be tipping us off to Adonijah's less-than-noble character by comparing him to Absalom.

- Like Absalom, Adonijah got "himself chariots and horsemen, and fifty men to run before him" (v. 5; cf. 2 Sam. 15:1).
- Like Absalom, Adonijah was "handsome" (v. 6; cf. 2 Sam. 14:25).
- Like Absalom and Amnon (2 Sam. 18:5; 13:21), sadly, Adonijah enjoyed a little too much of his father's favor (v. 6).

Adonijah also had a lot of powerful supporters on his side. There was Joab, David's nephew and commander of the army, and Abiathar, the co-high priest who had been with David since the massacre at Nob. With a military leader and a religious leader on his side, Adonijah posed a formidable threat.

But those not on Adonijah's side were more important than those who were. Zadok had been named co-high priest when David became king. Benaiah was the commander of the palace guards. Nathan the prophet had been David's faithful spiritual counselor, and he was joined in his resistance to Adonijah by all of David's mighty men.

As he witnessed Adonijah's actions unfold, Nathan the prophet was understandably concerned. He advised Bathsheba to act quickly, or her life and Solomon's would be in extreme jeopardy if Adonijah were to establish himself as David's successor. Bathsheba approached the king in his bedroom and informed him of Adonijah's deeds, of the feast he was hosting for all his allies and the sons of David, and of Solomon's lack of invitation.

According to the plan, Nathan entered the room to confirm all that Bathsheba had said and needled David into taking action. It is not an overstatement to say that this man of God stood in the gap at a pivotal moment in Israel's history and fearlessly ministered God's word to the throne as he had always done. It had been Nathan who had messengered God's promise to establish David's dynasty forever (2 Sam. 7:1-17); it had also been

Nathan who had confronted the tyrant over his adultery with Bathsheba and the murder of Uriah (2 Sam. 12:1-15). Nathan shrewdly knew which buttons in David needed pushing.

Nathan's cajoling had the intended effect. David instructed his aides to take Solomon to Gihon and anoint him king. David may have been in decline, but he was still a shrewd tactician and an expert in political theater. His instructions were carefully orchestrated to ensure that Adonijah's coup was stopped dead in its tracks, and the nation's heart did not swing to him as it had to Absalom.

Solomon was proclaimed king at a conspicuous landmark in Jerusalem. Gihon was a spring just outside of Jerusalem and the source of the city's water, so it was a perfect place to coronate a new sovereign. The route from the palace to the spring would have been one of Jerusalem's busiest streets, and the spring itself would have been like a city square, a natural public gathering place.

So great was the celebration over Solomon's anointing that the roar of the approving crowd could be heard about 650 yards south at En-rogel where Adonijah was still dining with his guests. Abiathar's son, Jonathan, enters the scene and explains to Adonijah and his guests what has transpired. David has stopped the coup in its tracks. Solomon is now the bona fide king; Adonijah's dream boat has been torpedoed. And that's when all of Adonijah's friends scattered.

Adonijah did what any persona non grata must do in that day; he fled to the horns of the altar of God and pled for mercy. When Adonijah gave his word to Solomon that he would not engage in any seditious activities, he was allowed to return home, meaning he was being forced to retire from public life, at least until he returned to Solomon's good graces.

Read 1 Kings 2. In his deathbed charge, David's comments echoed Deuteronomy. Particularly noteworthy is the command in Deuteronomy for the king to write out by hand a copy of the Law for his personal use (Deut. 17:18-19). Such an obligation would have reminded the king that he was not above the Law (Deut. 17:20). Solomon's fidelity to the Law was a concern for David because, though God had established David's throne forever, David knew that the success and longevity of the Davidic dynasty depended on his sons' obedience to the Law.

But after extolling Torah fidelity, David's charge takes a violent turn. First, he says, Joab must be executed. The dying king recalls what his right-hand man and former general had done by murdering Abner (2 Sam. 3:28-29) and Amasa (2 Sam. 19:13). "Do not let his gray head go down to Sheol in peace" (v. 6), a command that not only precluded natural death at a ripe old age, but also expressed the wish that Joab die outside of a right relationship with God. David desperately wanted to enjoy the afterlife far away from Joab, and he was afraid that Joab's blood-guilt would continue to haunt the royal family if not properly avenged (v. 5).

Also to be dealt with was Shimei, who had cursed David while on the run from Absalom (2 Sam. 16:5-12), and in ancient Israel, cursing the Lord's anointed was forbidden (Exod. 22:28). After being restored to the throne, David had sworn not to execute Shimei for his crime. But the oath did not in any way prohibit Solomon from doing the deed. As a member of the tribe of Benjamin—Saul's tribe—Shimei would continue to pose a threat.

In stark contrast to the fates of Joab and Shimei, David wished for Solomon to reward the loyalty of Barzillai, a wealthy landowner in Gilead who had provided David with badly-needed food and support during Absalom's insurrection (2 Sam. 17:24-29). It was commanded that Barzillai's family be invited to the king's table, effectively placing them on a royal pension of sorts.

After David's death, Bathsheba was approached by Adonijah. He begrudgingly acknowledged that Solomon was the legitimate king of Israel—"for it was his from the LORD"—but cannot give up the idea that it was still somehow rightfully his—"the kingdom was mine, and [...] all Israel fully expected me to reign" (v. 15). So as a consolation prize for losing the crown, Adonijah requested that Bathsheba ask Solomon to give Abishag, David's final concubine, to Adonijah as a wife.

Bathsheba consented to carrying Adonijah's request to the king. Any initial perception of Solomon as a docile momma's boy is shredded by a volcanic eruption of righteous indignation. The king immediately ordered the execution of his brother. Why? Because it was clear to Solomon that his older brother had not totally surrendered his claim to the throne or dream of being king (cf. 2 Sam. 3:6-7; 12:8; 16:21-22)—notice Solomon's words to Bathsheba, "You might as well request the kingdom for him" (v. 22 NIV).

After signing Adonijah's execution warrant, Solomon also sent the high priest Abiathar into exile. The narrator takes this opportunity to stress a prominent theme in Kings, that the Word of the Lord is always inevitably fulfilled. The demotion of Abiathar fulfilled the prophecy made about Eli's family (1 Sam. 2:27-36; 3:11-14)—Abiathar was the grandson of Ahitub, the grandson of Eli (cf. 1 Sam. 14:2-3; 22:20).

When Joab learned that Adonijah had been executed, he panicked and claimed sanctuary on the horns of the altar (just as Adonijah had done). His response to Benaiah, "I will die here" was meant in the same way as our sarcastic, "You can have it when you pry it from my cold dead fingers." Learning of Joab's response, Solomon said, "Have it your way."

Finally, Shimei, the former caretaker of Saul's estate, was summoned before the king. Solomon effectively convicted Shimei of manslaughter for his curse on David and appropriately sentenced him to house arrest in Jerusalem as if it were a city of refuge. The sentence was not to cross the Kidron Valley, which would have been necessary for Shimei to visit his hometown of Bahurim and have contact with his kin. It should be noted that Shimei consented to this restriction (v. 38).

After three years, two of Shimei's servants escaped to the Philistine city of Gath, about twenty-five miles southwest of Jerusalem. Shimei ventured out to fetch them back to service, but Solomon was waiting for Shimei when he returned. For breaking his oath to the king, to say nothing of his cursing David so many years before, Shimei was eliminated. The narrator's final words of the chapter, "So the kingdom was established in the hand of Solomon," effectively gives divine sanction to the king's punitive measures and establishes Solomon as a shrewd regent possessing extraordinary wisdom.

APPLICATION

Scars of Sin. "Sin makes cowards of us all." Whoever first said that was right. Beginning with his sin with Bathsheba in 2 Samuel 11, David's strong leadership slowly erodes, both in his family and in Israel. In 1 Kings 1, David is weak and indecisive at best. As with Amnon and Absalom, he was unable to discipline Adonijah. Only at the behest of Bathsheba and Nathan did he proclaim Solomon his successor. Sin makes cowards of us all, and that is never truer than for leaders. The moral courage required to make tough decisions evaporates as we cede more of our souls to Satan. There's a reason persistent sin gives cause for concern about a leader's character.

Courage to Forgive. It requires an exceptionally strong leader to extend grace and forgiveness. Adonijah begged his half-brother Solomon for mercy. No one in that age would have faulted Solomon for disposing of him at that point. But Solomon extended grace so long as Adonijah promised to behave himself (he didn't and was later executed anyway). Some leaders seem to think that strong leadership is exemplified by being punitive and harsh. But if God's discipline is always meant to correct and restore, what good do leaders achieve by simply being cruel? Extending grace and forgiveness is the most difficult thing a leader must do. However, grace and forgiveness are not signs of weakness, but of extraordinary strength.

The Final Score. A presumptuous Adonijah hosted a feast for his allies, but the party grew quite lame when the raucous celebration of Solomon's coronation was heard. Adonijah's "friends" fled in panic, and the premature victory feast grew cold. Jesus, too, has promised to share a feast with us (Matt. 26:29), one that will occur before the final battle and his kingdom has been established (Rev. 19). But this is not unfounded presumption, for we serve a Commander-in-Chief who has never known defeat. And just as Barzillai was seated at the king's table because of his faithfulness, we too will be given a seat at our Lord's feast if we are found faithful. As we gather around the Lord's table each Sunday to commemorate his death and anticipate his return, we shout with one voice: "Long live the King!"

CONCLUSION

As you read this sordid political tale of Adonijah's downfall and Solomon's ascendancy, you could be excused for asking, "Where is God in this?" Though he seems hidden, God was at work behind the scenes, manipulating human sinfulness to achieve his ultimate purposes. It was not necessarily his will that Adonijah and others behave the way they did, but God worked through them nonetheless.

For the Jews living in exile, this story affirmed that Israel's throne, and no less Israel herself, fell under the sovereign rule of God. For Christians, the opening narrative of Kings points the way to the King of kings whom God has established on his throne to rule in majesty and power forever. Throughout, we see how God worked his plan through (and in spite of) Israel's dirty politics.

QUESTIONS FOR REFLECTION

1. Why did David's aides bring him a young, beautiful virgin to "keep him warm"? What were they trying to accomplish?

2. What facts does the narrator give us about Adonijah that are intended to remind us of Absalom?

3. What man of God stepped up to make sure God's chosen successor for David was made king?

4. Why did David want Joab executed? Why had David himself never dealt with Joab?

5. Why did Solomon order Adonijah's execution?

6. What events in this story seem consistent with God's will? What events seem to go against God's will? Who is responsible for the story ending consistent with God's will—man or God?

QUESTIONS FOR DISCUSSION

1. How does sin slowly erode the moral fortitude of a leader?

2. Explain this statement: "Forgiveness is not for weak people."

3. In your opinion, did Adonijah, Joab, and Shimei deserve their fates? Did Abiathar? Why/why not?

4. What does this passage teach us about Christ and the church?

5. What hope does this story give God's people as we witness political events unfold in a way that seems inconsistent with God's will?

6. Because he was convinced of God's sovereign will, Nathan stepped forward in order for that will to transpire, instead of sitting back and "waiting on God." When is it appropriate to be proactive according to God's plan vs. "let go and let God"?

2

SOLOMON'S KINGDOM

1 KINGS 3-4

Objective: To observe Solomon's success as king,
but also note the origins of his fall

INTRODUCTION

With forty years on the throne, David had unequivocally established a dynasty. Now Solomon receives an unprecedented blessing from God as he begins his reign in 1 Kings 3. In 1 Kings 4, the details of Solomon's reign, though tedious, underscore just how successful he was. Solomon gets a lot of love from the narrator in this section. But we need to bear in mind that the glory of Solomon came at a cost. As you read these chapters, you'll be tempted to think nothing could go wrong for Solomon. But all is not exactly well in Camelot.

EXAMINATION

Read 1 Kings 3:1-15. If the Lord came to you in a dream and promised you anything you wanted, what would you request? All the money in the world? All the power in the world? Would you ask for your health to be made perfect? Would you wish for a spouse? Children? A new job?

While at Gibeon, Solomon had a dream in which God offered to grant him a wish. Solomon had just become king. He had subdued enemies of his throne. But the immensity of the responsibility before Solomon weighed on his heart. As he thought of his God and his people, Solomon knew he had big shoes to fill.

The king then confessed to God that he felt as "but a little child" and did "not know how to go out or come in" (v. 7). It had been only about seventy years since Israel had switched from a loose confederacy of tribes to a monarchy, and that transition had been rocky. Meanwhile, Israel's population had continued to explode, and Solomon knew that Israel needed a leader who would excel in administration (cf. v. 9).

More importantly, and from a spiritual perspective, Solomon recognized a king's ability to become stubborn and hard-hearted vs. discerning. Rather than becoming deaf to the divine word and blind to his need for divine aid, Solomon wanted to remain sensitive to God's guidance and direction. Power corrupts; absolute power corrupts absolutely; and the first thing to go is often a self-awareness of one's own inadequacies. The king's humility is remarkable. He understood the enormous responsibility before him; what is more, he knew discharging his duty faithfully and successfully required divine help.

The Lord was pleased with Solomon's humble request. In addition to extraordinary, unprecedented wisdom, the Lord gave the king unprecedented "riches and honor, so that no other king shall compare with you" (v. 13). In addition, Solomon would receive lengthened days (i.e., a long life) if he were faithful to the covenant.

Solomon returned to Jerusalem and threw a sumptuous feast for his ministers and aides, a celebration of God's blessing on the new king. For now, the Lord is unequivocally Solomon's choice of gods, and Solomon is unequivocally God's choice of king.

Read 1 Kings 3:16-28. Without question, this is the most famous story from Solomon's reign. We've just learned that Solomon's wisdom has a divine source; this episode is presented as an anecdote of such wisdom. More specifically, this story is representative not only of how Solomon shrewdly adjudicated cases brought before him, but also how he did so without bias concerning the social standing of the contestants. In other words, the story proved Solomon was as compassionate as he was smart.

No matter how moral a society may be, prostitution will always have its customers, and this was certainly true of ancient Israel, despite it being outlawed (Lev. 19:29; Deut. 23:18). The profession of these two women is meant to arouse more sympathy than shame—prostitutes became such by being sold into the lifestyle by their parents or themselves because they had no other means of financial support. These two women were at the bottom of their social hierarchy, the least likely to receive (let alone deserve) justice.

The first woman relates to the king a tragic story of two births, a midnight accident while the women were alone (i.e., without "customers," but also making this a "she said, she said" issue), a swapping of infants, and ambiguity as to which woman is the birth mother of the surviving child. Not even the narrator means for us to know who is telling the truth—we merely assume that the first woman speaks the truth, but on what basis (cf. Prov. 18:17)? If there had been a second witness who could corroborate one side or the other, the legal process could have played out (Deut. 19:15). But of course, there wasn't, and it couldn't.

Solomon's famous solution was to cut the Gordian knot by splitting the child in two with a sword—a solution that abhorred the actual mother, instantly giving the king the answer to the question. Later, Solomon would speak of how "a king who sits on the throne of judgment winnows all evil with his eyes" (Prov. 20:8), and that though God conceals certain things, "the glory of kings is to search things out" (Prov. 25:2). Indeed, while David had been the Lord's mighty man of war on the throne, Solomon would be his all-wise and discerning administrator of Israel.

Read 1 Kings 4. David was arguably Israel's greatest king, but it doesn't seem as if he had had much of a domestic agenda. Rather, he was always off fighting wars with one enemy or another. But Solomon had successfully secured his kingdom in peace, to say nothing of having received a remarkable endowment of divine wisdom. Thus, this chapter goes on to demonstrate how Solomon went about establishing a sound government so that the affairs of the nation were adequately addressed. In the early verses of the chapter, we are introduced to his cabinet:

- Zadok's grandson, Azariah, was the high priest. His father was presumably still alive and likely serving in an emeritus position since he is mentioned in v. 4.

- Solomon's two secretaries, Elihoreph and Ahijah, enjoyed very high positions in the government, second only to the master of the palace. One may have been a secretary or minister of inter-national relations, while the other was over internal or domestic affairs, as was done in Assyria.

- The recorder, Jehoshaphat, functioned as a "royal herald." He brought public needs to the king's attention and then turned around and served as the king's spokesman or press secretary (cf. 2 Kgs 18:18). It's possible that his duties also included that of a state prosecutor or attorney general.

- Benaiah was Solomon's top military commander.

- Azariah, the son of Nathan the prophet, "was over the officers," meaning the governors set over the administrative districts in Israel (vv. 7-19).

- Nathan's other son, Zabud, "was priest and king's friend." This last position was likely that of chief personal advisor to Solomon, not unlike a combination of the White House's chief of staff and the president's personal chaplain.

- Next is Ahishar, the palace overseer or head servant, and Adoni-ram, chief of corvée or forced labor.

Solomon divided Israel into a dozen administrative districts, with of-ficers or governors in charge of each. For one month each year, a district was responsible for feeding the royal household. Solomon's twelve districts were somewhat based on old tribal territories, but not rigidly. Solomon again demonstrates his administrative acumen by redrawing district lines in his favor. Conspicuously absent from the list is any mention of the tribe or territory of Judah, which may have been exempted from taxation.

The narrator succinctly expresses the point of the second half of 1 Kings 4 with "Judah and Israel were as many as the sand by the sea. They ate and drank and were happy" (v. 19). Surprising as it might be, this is the first time in the Old Testament that this statement is made about Israel as a pres-ent reality. Only now was God's promise to Abraham fulfilled—"I will surely bless you, and I will surely multiply your offspring as the stars of heaven and as the sand that is on the seashore" (Gen. 22:17). Not even under David's leadership did Israel realize the Abrahamic promise to this degree.

It was also under Solomon's watch that Israel's territory finally ex-panded to encompass all that God had promised the patriarch. "Solomon ruled over all the kingdoms from the Euphrates to the land of the Philistines and to the border of Egypt" (v. 21; cf. Gen. 12:1-9; 15:18; Exod. 23:31; Deut. 11:24; Josh. 1:4).

The remainder of the passage expresses the narrator's gushing admiration for the glory days of Solomon. On any given day, the king's table required 180 bushels of flour, 360 bushels of meal, 10 oxen, 20 cattle, 100 sheep, and assorted deer, gazelles, roebucks, and birds. Surely, Solomon's daily dining table redefined the phrase "a meal fit for a king! And his stables full of horses and horsemen weren't too shabby, either (vv. 26-28).

To the king's personal largesse is added a statement about the dominion he enjoyed over so expansive a territory and the peace he oversaw. The vassals he had inherited from his father continued to honor him with lavish tribute. "From Dan even to Beersheba" (v. 25; cf. "from sea to shining sea"), Israel was safe and secure. Surely this peace was due to the other-worldly wisdom God had bestowed on his royal servant.

Solomon was the author of 3,000 proverbs, of which the book of Proverbs contains about 582 by one count. He is said to have been wiser than the Egyptians, even wiser than the Einsteins of his day. Solomon also had an interest in and drew insight from his observations of botany and zoology. Similar to Nebuchadnezzar's Hanging Gardens some four centuries later, Solomon might have cultivated a large, impressive botanical garden near his palace.

This passage gushes with praise to God for keeping his promises. In the Old Testament, living in safety under a vine and fig tree (v. 25) indicated a long life pregnant with the covenant blessings (cf. Deut. 12:10; Joel 2:22; Mic. 4:4; Zech. 3:10). In virtually every conceivable way, Israel under Solomon enjoyed all the blessings promised to them in the Sinai covenant.

APPLICATION

Bold Prayers. You and I will never be as rich, wise, or powerful as Solomon. But the same God who so generously gave to Solomon when he prayed remains the God who hears the prayers of all his people and answers generously. In prayer, Jesus taught us to ask, seek, and knock in order to receive good gifts from our Father (Matt. 7:7, 11; 21:22; John 14:13-14). God gives above and beyond our wildest imaginations (Eph. 3:20). But some people never experience the fullness of their Father's generosity, either because they are unwilling to work for it, or because they never ask (Jas. 4:2). In Solomon's prayer at Gibeon, he models for us how we ought to approach God. 1) He acknowledged God's past action, 2) he asked for God's continued blessing, 3) he expressed humility, and, finally, 4) he asked for the strength to do God's will.

Wise Leadership. There is arguably no greater trait so essential to effective leadership than wisdom (cf. Acts 6:3). Biblical wisdom is not heightened intellect, strong secular education, common sense, or a commanding knowledge of Scripture; biblical wisdom encompasses a right relationship with God and knowing in one moment to the next what will be pleasing to God. Despite all the sage advice he left behind in Proverbs, Solomon proved a failure at following much of his own counsel. Some leaders may be "book smart," have impressive credentials, possess business savvy, talk a good game, or even be fluent in Scripture. But none of these things can prevent them from proving to be fools when and where it matters most. As we attempt to discern wisdom in potential leaders, we ought to ask, "Does this person seek wisdom for wisdom's sake, or to draw nearer to God and bless the lives of others?"

Ignoring Caution Signs. For anyone who knows the rest of the story, the note that Solomon married an Egyptian (3:1) sounds an ominous tone at the beginning of his reign. Intermarrying with the Gentiles proved to be the beginning of the end of Solomon's reign and Israel's decline. Sadly, our success often blinds us to our spiritual blunders until it's too late. It's not unlike taking on a curve on a windy road at a high rate of speed. Most of the time, one can enter a curve in the road and safely leave unheeded the warning sign to slow down. But it only takes one ignored caution and one curve taken too fast to lead to our death, and our folly will be realized too late. Better to obey and leave the consequences to God than to consider his laws as "no big deal" and see our kingdom slip away.

CONCLUSION

To be honest, I'm not sure what to think about Solomon. Most of this section describes with sincere admiration the glory of Solomon's giftedness and empire. Solomon was wise and skilled at so many things, yet he ultimately failed to discover the end of all wisdom—uninterrupted fellowship with the Lord. In reality, Solomon had just enough wisdom to make it to the top of the totem pole in his world, but not enough to teach him to rely on the Lord for all things.

Christians can rejoice that one greater than Solomon has come (Matt. 12:42). In him, Paul says, "are hidden all the treasures of wisdom and knowledge" (Col. 2:3). Isn't it impressive (and just a bit outlandish?) that God offers members of his kingdom a glory greater than Solomon ever had? If God cares so much about the flora and fauna of earth—of which Solomon knew so much—how will he also not provide for our every need in Christ? Seek first God's kingdom, and you'll discover something of which Solomon could only dream.

QUESTIONS FOR REFLECTION

1. What did Solomon ask of the Lord at Gibeon? What did he receive from the Lord?

2. Name the four components of Solomon's prayer.

3. Why was Israel in such desperate need of a firm administrator at this point in her history?

4. What point does the story of Solomon "splitting the baby" tell us about Solomon, his wisdom, and his character?

5. Into how many districts did Solomon divide Israel? Which tribe was exempt?

6. What statements are made in 1 Kings 4 about Israel's peace and prosperity during Solomon's reign?

7. What significant statement is made in v. 21 about the size of Israel's territory? Why is the statement important?

QUESTIONS FOR DISCUSSION

1. What details about Solomon in 1 Kings 3-4 do you find troubling or do you believe portend future disaster?

2. What prevents people from being bold in their prayers?

3. What does biblical wisdom encompass?

4. What traits do people *normally* look for in potential leaders What traits should Christians *ideally* look for in potential leaders?

5. Was it a sin for Solomon to marry an Egyptian? Defend your answer.

6. Read 1 Corinthians 6:12. How could Solomon have benefited from this wise counsel?

7. What sort of things should Christian beware of, even though they might not technically be a sin?

3

SOLOMON'S TEMPLE
1 KINGS 5-8

Objective: To consider Solomon's Temple
and its implications for the New Testament temple

INTRODUCTION

In ancient times, temples were always at the center of a developed society, and the construction and maintenance of them was the purview of the king. To some, studying 1 Kings 5-8 will be as exciting as watching grass grow. But it is important that we consider Solomon's Temple, its importance to Israel, and the role it plays in the story of 1-2 Kings. Though it was worthy of care as God's house, Israel eventually put too much emphasis on the Temple at the expense of its Owner, and as we will see, this provides a cautionary tale for God's people today.

EXAMINATION

Read 1 Kings 5. The city of Tyre was located about fifty miles north of Jerusalem. David and Hiram, king of Tyre, had been allies, and David had previously contracted with him to supply Israel with building materials for the Temple (2 Sam. 5:11). Since Hiram constructed three impressive temples of his own, he would have known how to help.

Having established his kingdom, Solomon sent a request to Hiram for the building materials David had first solicited. Solomon proposed that both Solomon's and Hiram's servants be used in the venture, with Solomon footing the bill. Thus began the process of building a permanent place for God in Israel, a prophecy made by Moses several times in Deuteronomy.

Hiram had logs of the famed Cedars of Lebanon floated down to Joppa as rafts, then broken apart and shipped inland to Jerusalem. In return, Solomon paid Hiram an annual stipend in agricultural produce: over 800 tons of grain and more than 100,000 gallons of pure olive oil, neither of which were available in the area of Tyre. From all appearances, no expense was spared in securing materials for the Temple, and such a fact highlights the building's importance to Solomon.

To assist with the logging, Solomon drafted thirty thousand Canaanites to work in Lebanon in one-month-on/two-months-off shifts. To prepare the raw materials for the Temple's construction, Solomon conscripted an additional 150,000 workers in Israel, all overseen by 3,300 officials. Stonecutters were especially valuable in this enterprise—away from the Temple site, they had to prepare the stones (some of them seven feet in size) and fit them together without mortar like an intricate puzzle.

In this way, Solomon procured the supplies necessary to build the Temple. He proved himself to be a master negotiator. God's blessing was indeed great on Solomon's administration. Soon, the Lord would have a house of his own in the Promised Land.

Read 1 Kings 6-7. The capital city of Jerusalem that Solomon inherited from his father was rather small by today's standards, occupying just twelve acres. It thus did not have room for a larger royal residence or the Temple, so the entire complex was constructed to the north of the old city upon Mount Moriah, on what had been Araunah's threshing floor.

The measurements of the Temple are given as sixty cubits long, twenty cubits wide, and forty cubits high. Compare this to the Tabernacle, which was a hundred cubits long, fifty cubits wide, and more than eight cubits high—the dimensions of the Tabernacle, though larger, included the courtyard. Take away the Tabernacle's courtyard, and the Temple was nearly double its size. Also, the Temple was more than three times the height of the Tabernacle (about fourteen feet), towering five stories or nearly sixty feet above the surrounding landscape.

The Temple's basic design was long and narrow and included:

- a vestibule or entry hall
- a main hall measuring approximately 1,700 square feet
- an inner sanctuary (the Most Holy Place) measuring 850 square feet
- side rooms (for storage, presumably) off the main hall
- windows with "recessed frames"
- frame and beams of Lebanon cedars provided by Hiram

The ancient Israelites were very sensitive to maintaining holiness in a particular place. Thus, the note that no hammers, axes, or other iron tools were used on the construction site (v. 7) speaks to the sacredness of the Temple grounds. The work was done at the original location, and the finished product was only then brought onto the site.

To highlight the uniqueness of this building, we should also note that gold was very predominant throughout the building, as were images of gourds, flowers, and palm trees. In ancient Near Eastern symbology, the palm tree represented fertility and the tree of life, and the totality of the carved images of flora was meant to conjure an image of paradise.

Cherubim were also particularly prominent in the Most Holy Place, where they rose to half the height of the actual room and their wings towered over the space. In Scripture, cherubs always represented God's presence; they were part of the divine entourage in ancient thinking. Ezekiel's description of cherubim (Ezek. 1:4-14) affirms that cherubs are large and fearsome, and nothing like the cute baby cherubs preserved in Valentine's Day cards or Renaissance art.

Though the Temple took over seven years to build, the narrator seems to be a bit offended that Solomon took twice as long to build a new royal residence (7:1). The palace complex was known as "the House of the Forest of Lebanon," both because of the abundance of cedar that adorned the residence (much more than the Temple), and because of the four rows of cedar columns that made the palace resemble an actual cedar forest in Lebanon. This first house at times served as both a large assembly or reception hall and also an armory.

Included in the palace was the Hall of Pillars, but its use is not stated. There was also the Hall of the Throne where Solomon sat enthroned and adjudicated cases brought before him. Next came his dwelling and that of his Egyptian wife. The entire complex was decorated with expensive stonework and ornamented in cedar.

But our tour guide does not linger long here. Returning to the Temple, we learn that Solomon brought in a gifted sculptor of bronze, an Israelite of Naphtali (7:13-14). This Hiram of Tyre is not to be confused with King Hiram, whom Solomon solicited for help with the Temple's raw materials. Though he was from Tyre, this Hiram is clearly an Israelite through his mother. Like Bezalel and Oholiab, who worked on the Tabernacle, Hiram is said to have been divinely gifted in wisdom and skill for his craft.

It was he who designed and cast the two free-standing pillars of Solomon's Temple, Jachin and Boaz. Both were nearly three stories in height, eighteen feet in circumference, and, though hollow inside, the metal was four fingers thick.

The large bronze sea, or water tank, in the Temple courtyard was over fourteen feet in diameter and seven feet high; it sat upon a stand of a dozen oxen (possibly reflecting the twelve tribes), three pointing in each direction. The sea could hold 12,000 gallons of water (the average backyard, in-ground pool holds 18,000-20,000 gallons).

Hiram made ten mobile stands of bronze, richly ornamented, and upon these stands rested ten bronze basins, each holding 240 gallons of water (the average household hot water heater holds 60-80 gallons). These stands and their basins were placed on either side of the Temple and used for rinsing/washing purposes.

Hiram also cast in bronze the various pots and utensils used in Temple service by the priests. But note that Solomon is given credit for the sacred vessels made of gold, including the altar, table, and ten golden lampstands. Upon completion, into the Temple's storerooms Solomon brought immense treasures first collected and dedicated to the Lord by David.

Read 1 Kings 8. The Temple now completed, Solomon instructed that the Ark be brought to its new home. With great fanfare and innumerable sacrifices, the Ark and the holy vessels were placed in the Temple, with the Ark specifically in the Most Holy Place. In the history of the Ark, God's presence had always been associated with it in a very powerful, very tangible way. So when the Ark had arrived at the Temple, a cloud—symbolic of the Lord's glory—filled the Temple to the point that the priests could not perform their duties. Such was affirmation of divine approval for what Solomon had accomplished. Solomon's blessing on the people assembled (vv. 13-21) invoked three important ideas.

1. God's covenant with David was an outgrowth of God's covenant with Israel at Sinai (vv. 16-17). God's favor to the House of David was only a part of his grander favor to the children of Abraham, Isaac, and Jacob.

2. Solomon explained why there had been a delay in building the Temple in the Promised Land (vv. 18-19). David had desired to build it, and God had commended him for the desire, but had reserved such an honor for Solomon. By noting God's allowing Solomon to build the Temple, the king is reminding the people that he is God's anointed.

3. The king celebrated how the Temple would house both the Ark and God's Name (vv. 20-21). Because the Temple houses both God's Ark and God's Name, it is unique and to be venerated.

Solomon's subsequent prayer (vv. 22-53) is important to our understanding of the rest of Kings. Much of it is rooted in the covenant blessings/curses found in Leviticus 26 and Deuteronomy 27-28. In his opening remarks of this prayer, Solomon confessed that the God of Israel was unique and beyond comparison to any other god (vv. 23-24) and asked that God be faithful to his covenant with David and, barring disobedience, see to it that a son of David occupied Israel's throne forever (vv. 25-26). He also requested that the prayers of many offered in and toward the Temple might be answered by Israel's God (vv. 27-53).

Concerning this last request, Solomon went on to make seven more requests concerning prayers in the Temple:

1. Hear the prayer of one who is falsely accused (vv. 31-32). Some court cases would prove too difficult to solve, so Solomon asked God to adjudicate these and vindicate the righteous.

2. Hear the prayer of Israel when she is defeated and repents (vv. 33-34). Recall that military defeat as punishment for sin was among the covenant curses (Lev. 26:33; Deut. 28:36-37).

3. Hear the prayer of Israel when she suffers drought (vv. 35-36), which was also among the covenant curses (Lev. 26:19; Deut. 11:13-17; 28:23-24).

4. Hear the prayer of Israel when she suffers famine or plague (vv. 37-40). These are also echoed in the covenant curses (Deut. 28:21-22, 27, 35, 38-39, 42, 59-61).

5. Hear the prayer of a foreigner in order to glorify yourself to the ends of the earth (vv. 41-43). It is in this request that Solomon's prayer takes on a more international tone.

6. Hear the prayer of Israel when she goes to war (vv. 44-45). In ancient warfare, people believed that a battle between two nations was merely a physical parallel to war in the divine realm between the nation's two patron deities. Thus, Solomon is asking that God vindicate his people by vindicating himself whenever Israel took up the sword.

7. Hear the prayer of Israel in Exile and restore her to the Promised Land (vv. 46-51; cf. Deut. 28:36-37, 58-68). This final request is striking because it seems to presuppose that the people will not be faithful, that Exile is inevitable.

After Solomon's prayer, he stood and blessed the people again (vv. 56-61). The final verse of the chapter, "[the people] went to their homes joyful and glad of heart for all the goodness that the LORD had shown to David his servant and to Israel his people" (v. 66), is a perfect summary of God's enormous blessing on Israel.

APPLICATION

Worship: Horizontal and Vertical. Embedded in Solomon's Temple prayer is a reminder that God is glorified when there is harmony with one another (8:31-32). But throughout Israel's history, loving one's neighbor often took a back seat, to the point that God spurned Israel's sacrifices (Amos 5:21-24; cf. Hos. 6:6). Jesus reminds us that our worship is rejected when it comes from a heart that is not at peace with one's fellow man (Matt. 5:23-24). This is why Jesus considered the two greatest commandments—love God and love your neighbor—to be of equal importance.

No Forgiveness? It is often claimed that there was no forgiveness of sins in the Old Testament. But a key theme of Solomon's prayer is Israel's repentance (vv. 31-53). The Temple is considered as a place to which the people of God must turn when they seek forgiveness, healing, and restoration. The notion that God would not forgive his people is entirely foreign from this text; Solomon depicts the Lord as a heavenly Father eager and willing to forgive his people when they seek his face. In the New Testament, our prayer for forgiveness is also addressed to God via the new "temple," the person of Christ. In both Testaments, then, we can clearly see that God is "not wishing for any to perish but for all to come to repentance" (2 Pet. 3:9 NASU).

Lucky Rabbit's Foot. Even after the Babylonian Exile, the Jews continued to invest too much in the Temple, seeing it as a lucky charm of sorts, something that would guarantee their survival (cf. John 11:48). Sadly, however, they rejected Jesus (the new temple), precipitating their end as a nation. Today, church buildings are not integral to the church's survival. Rather, it is Jesus that is integral to our survival and success. More than a temple, Jesus is now our great high priest and our great sacrifice (Heb. 9-10). Christians must take care that they do not turn their buildings into idols. Temples and church buildings are only a means to an end; Christ is the end.

CONCLUSION

The importance of the Temple to Israel's self-identity can hardly be overstated. Throughout the rest of the Old Testament, the Temple was a reminder of God's sovereignty, his deserving of worship, and the need for Israel to be faithful. In good times and bad, the Temple always represented God's judgment on the nation, as well as a call to rededication.

In the same way, church buildings for Christians can remind us of God's faithfulness and blessing. But they cannot become idols as the Temple eventually did for Israel. The Temple never housed the physical presence of God, but was intended to remind Israel of God's spiritual presence with his people. In the same way, church buildings are not holy because they contain God's physical presence, but should be used to the glory of the Son of God, the true New Testament temple.

QUESTIONS FOR REFLECTION

1. How does 1 Kings 5-8 further demonstrate Solomon's wisdom?

2. Why did workmen not use iron tools at the Temple building site?

3. What happened when the Ark was brought into the Temple?

4. What seven things did Solomon petition God for in his prayer at the Temple dedication?

QUESTIONS FOR DISCUSSION

1. What happens when we put too much emphasis on our vertical relationship with God and not enough on our relationships with others?

2. Was there forgiveness of sins in the Old Testament? If so, how is this a greater truth for those living under the new covenant?

3. How have you seen congregations have an unhealthy view of or affection for their church building? What can be done to keep church buildings from becoming idols?

4. Is the church building inherent to "doing church"? Can you see a time in the future when churches might not be able to afford buildings? If so, in what ways will churches need to adapt?

4

SOLOMON'S FALL

1 KINGS 9-11

Objective: To discover the factors that
led to Solomon's spiritual downfall

INTRODUCTION

The glory of Solomon's kingdom was indeed impressive. But there were
cracks in the golden veneer. Carl DeVries makes the excellent observation
that Solomon's "gradual apostasy had more disastrous results than the infa-
mous scandal of his father, who sincerely repented." The key phrase in that
statement is "gradual apostasy," vs. the momentary failure of David. In all
the annals of following the Lord and spiritual living, it has been the slow
fade—not the sudden fall—that has proven most devastating.

EXAMINATION

Read 1 Kings 9. Following the completion of Solomon's building projects
(including the palace and the Temple), "the LORD appeared to Solomon a
second time, as he had appeared to him at Gibeon" (v. 2). We have not yet
read any explicit condemnation of Solomon.

But note this phrase in v. 1—"all that Solomon desired to build." Solomon's building projects were near and dear to his heart, his life's passion, and at their completion, God saw fit to come to him as an intervention of sorts. The Hebrew term translated "desired" primarily refers to a physical attachment, but can also refer to a man desiring a woman (Gen. 34:8; Deut. 21:11), God's love for his people (Deut. 7:17; 10:15), and our reciprocal love for God (Psa. 91:14). That it is used here of Solomon's construction projects should give us pause.

The Lord reaffirmed the covenant he had made previously with David, including the reminder that judgment and wrath awaited if Solomon turned away from following God (vv. 6-7). Notably, God warned that, should Solomon and his sons be unfaithful to the covenant, he would turn Solomon's Temple into "a heap of ruins" and the people of Israel would become "a proverb and a byword" among the nations.

In some ways, the reaffirmation God gives to Solomon in these nine verses is intended to remind us of the special arrangement God had with the Davidic dynasty. But with its emphasis on the consequences should Solomon and the people prove unfaithful, this reaffirmation becomes an introduction to all that is about to transpire.

The remainder of this chapter will remind us of 1 Kings 4-5. In v. 11, we are told Solomon gave twenty Galilean cities to Hiram. Generous indeed, we are intended to think, especially when we realize this area contained a lot of fertile agricultural land. Upon inspection, however, Hiram discovered they were worthless. Much more problematic than whether Solomon gave Hiram a lemon is the notion that an Israelite king, the Lord's anointed, effectively deeded some of the Promised Land back to a Canaanite king! Several other ominous tones are sounded in this section:

- *Canaanites still in the land* (v. 21). God wanted them exterminated (Deut. 7:2; 20:17) because their continued presence would inevitably corrupt Israel's faith. Since they had been allowed to remain, Solomon put them to work. But disobedience, no matter the reason, is still disobedience.

- *Pharaoh's daughter* (vv. 16, 24; cf. 3:1; 7:8; 11:1). The narrator's continued fascination with Pharaoh's daughter is a warning of things to come, the "gateway drug" for Solomon's immoral addiction.

- *Accumulation of gold* (vv. 11, 14, 28). The amount of gold seems to increase rapidly, and Solomon continues to seek it out in more exotic locations. Whereas prosperity had once been measured by an abundance of food (4:20-23), it now seems to be illustrated with the abundance of gold.

- *Slave labor* (vv. 15-22). Using his force of conscripted labor, Solomon engaged in several building projects besides that of the Temple and a new royal palace.

With so many slaves at his disposal, Solomon became increasingly ambitious in his building projects. The identification of the Millo (vv. 15, 24) isn't absolutely certain, but it was likely a tower or bastion filling a vulnerable place in Jerusalem's wall.

Despite the twenty Galilean cities, Hiram and Solomon did very well as partners in accumulating wealth. Since Solomon controlled the important port city of Ezion-geber on the Red Sea, he ordered a fleet of trading ships be built and Hiram contributed veteran seaman. From Ophir, Solomon obtained sixteen tons of gold. In no uncertain terms, Solomon was a master at foreign trade.

Read 1 Kings 10. At the outset of Solomon's reign, God had promised the king "both riches and honor, so that no other king shall compare with you" (3:13; cf. 4:29-34). Now, to illustrate the level of fame and notoriety Solomon had achieved, the narrator tells us that the queen of Sheba came for a visit. With her impressive entourage, the queen came to test Solomon with questions. To all these and more, Solomon answered in a way that blew her away; "there was nothing hidden from the king that he could not explain to her" (v. 3). Add to that the king's palace, his dining table and officials and servants, his wardrobe, to say nothing of the Temple itself—all of the wining and dining stole the queen's breath away (v. 5).

In response, the queen blessed Solomon's God for giving the king such wealth, wisdom, and success. She then left behind an unprecedented gift of 120 gold talents—the same amount received from Hiram (9:14)—as well as spices, jewels, and gems. The cumulative effect of these gifts was that the queen was expressing her inferiority to Israel's king (v. 10; cf. Gen. 14:20). To reciprocate, Solomon gave her whatever she asked, in addition to the diplomatic gifts she had already received from the royal storehouses (v. 13).

A final time, we are told in the rest of the chapter some anecdotes stressing Solomon's splendor. The amount of gold listed in v. 14 (likely a total from 9:14, 9:28, and 10:10) did not include that gained from tolls and tariffs on maritime exploration and trade and from tax revenues from kings and governors under Solomon (v. 15). With this gold, Solomon had decorative shields made and hung them in the royal reception hall, the House of the Forest of Lebanon. So great was Solomon's accumulation of gold that "silver was not considered as anything in the days of Solomon" (v. 21). Later, we learn silver was as common as rocks in Solomon's day (v. 27).

Solomon sat atop an ornate throne of ivory, covered in gold and placed at the top of six steps, with lions on both sides of each step. The "ships of Tarshish" (v. 22) is a reference to a type of ship, and a large oceangoing vessel at that, one that could sustain multi-year voyages (compared to smaller ships that could only successfully navigate the Mediterranean).

Solomon continued to receive visitors to his kingdom, those wishing to hear and see for themselves the king's wisdom and glory. From these visitors, he received even *more* gifts and tribute—precious metals, clothing, spices, and livestock. He also increased his military hardware with chariots and horsemen (v. 26). He imported horses from Egypt and Kue; the details of this last transaction (v. 29) again depict Solomon as a master at international commerce.

Read 1 Kings 11. Finally, the narrator explicitly informs us that Solomon has not been as faithful to the Lord as he should have been. The king's downfall began with his passion for "foreign women." Besides his wife from Egypt, he also had wives from Moab, Ammon, Edom, Sidon, and the Hittites—all neighbors of Israel and each marriage likely a calculated political move. But whatever these unions did for Israel's national security or prestige, the narrator considers them to have been a violation of Deuteronomy 7:3-4. That Solomon loved these foreign women (v. 1) contrasts harshly with his love for God (3:3). On the Mount of Olives east of Jerusalem, Solomon built shrines to the false gods of his wives.

In both the warnings of Deuteronomy and the promises of the Davidic covenant (2 Sam. 7:14), God had sworn to discipline the king and his people when they became unfaithful. Sure enough, because of Solomon's apostasy, "the LORD was angry" (v. 9). And lest we think God was being too hard on Solomon, we must note that he has not violated some itty bitty, legal minutia in the Law of Moses, but rather the first two commandments of Sinai (Exod. 20:3-6). We are also reminded that the Lord had appeared to the king *twice* (v. 9) and warned him about idolatry—no excuses remained.

As punishment, God swore to tear a majority of the kingdom away from the house of David, but not during Solomon's lifetime. And it would not be the entire kingdom; a tribe would be left "for the sake of David my servant and for the sake of Jerusalem that I have chosen" (v. 13). To discipline Solomon, God raised up three adversaries against him. Whereas we had previously been told about the extraordinary peace that existed in Solomon's day (5:4), now we are to see violence and unrest plaguing his reign.

The first of these was Hadad of Edom (vv. 14-22). David had subjugated Edom (2 Sam. 8:13-14), and Joab had remained behind to purge the nation of every male survivor. But Hadad, a prince of Edom and only a small child, had escaped with members of his father's administration. Pharaoh offered him political asylum, allowed him to marry into the royal family of Egypt, and nurtured his hatred toward Israel. When Solomon ascended his father's throne, Hadad returned to Edom and eventually became a thorn in Solomon's side.

The second adversary was Rezon of Damascus (vv. 23-25). Nursing a bitter hatred against David, he had fled from the land of Zobah. After gathering a band of guerrillas, he overthrew Israel's garrison in Damascus (2 Sam. 8:6) and became the city's king. From Rezon and his people would rise the Syrians, a nation that would continually harass Israel for the next two centuries until finally subdued by the Assyrians.

The third adversary will become a greater character in the next chapter of Kings—Jeroboam of Ephraim (vv. 26-40). One day, as Jeroboam was leaving Jerusalem, he was approached by Ahijah of Shiloh. Ahijah took the new garment he wore and tore it into twelve pieces, symbolizing the tribes of Israel. He informed Jeroboam that God was giving him ten of the tribes, retaining "one" for the house of David. The twelfth tribe unaccounted for here was either Benjamin (which eventually went with Judah), Simeon (already assimilated into Judah), or Levi (always without territory). Eventually, Solomon put a bounty on Jeroboam's head, forcing the latter to flee to Egypt and seek asylum under Shishak.

The reign of Solomon is brought to a close by the narrator in a form that will become standard for many of the kings that follow him. The narrator refers us to the royal archives for more information, his total years of service are given, and we are informed of his burial.

APPLICATION

Pursuit of Riches. The extent to which Solomon went to increase the riches of his kingdom offers a warning to us. We live in one of the wealthiest nations on earth. Many of us own successful businesses, have enjoyed prosperous careers, live in beautiful homes, drive nice cars, and have closets full of attractive clothes. Our church culture often emphasizes that we are to give our best to God. But too often, this prudent maxim is manipulated into an excuse to show off before others. "Give my best to God" can become "dress to impress." "Look at how God has blessed me" can be an acceptable way of saying, "Look at how much I have achieved." Our false piety may fool others, but it will not fool God, who knows our hearts.

Young & Old. It is with tremendous sadness that we witness Solomon's slide into apostasy. Though it is certainly true that many walk away from the Lord in their youth, it's also true that we can lose our faithful fervor as we age (Eccles. 12:1). For the young, Solomon's life is a warning that following Jesus becomes more difficult as we age, not less. For the old, Solomon's life should prompt a moment's pause before criticizing the younger generation at the risk of ignoring a plank in one's own eye (Matt. 7:3-5). It is easier to trust the Lord when you have nothing; faith is an altogether different proposition when you are old, have accomplished much, are secure in your career or retirement, and are in need of nothing (cf. Deut. 8:10-14).

Marry in the Lord. Solomon's many wives and concubines offer a warning not to be yoked with unbelievers (2 Cor. 6:14). It is not a sin to marry a non-Christian, but just because something isn't sinful doesn't mean it's not unwise. Solomon's great-great-grandson, Jehoshaphat, established an alliance with Ahab and gave his son, Joram, in marriage to Ahab's daughter, Athaliah, and her reign of terror will be documented in 2 Kings 11. Simply put, marrying someone who does not share our spiritual values creates a lot of headaches and heartaches, just as it did for ancient Israel.

CONCLUSION

To a secular reader of Israel's history, Solomon was the nation's greatest king bar none and the one by whom all subsequent kings should be measured. Still, the standard would prove to be his father. Solomon will not be the last king in Jerusalem to fail to live up to the standard of David (v. 4). Indeed, only Hezekiah and Josiah are considered to have been equals with the famed giant killer.

In what is arguably the worst irony of his life, Solomon's pursuit of peace and wisdom did not pay the dividends we would expect, and it was because he did not pursue the Lord above all else. And for all the wisdom that was embodied in this son of David, Solomon ended up living out precious little of it.

QUESTIONS FOR REFLECTION

1. According to 9:1, what did Solomon "desire." How is this an ominous warning?

2. What other clues in 1 Kings 9-10 are precursors of Solomon's eventual unfaithfulness?

3. How was the Queen of Sheba's visit an "exclamation mark" on Solomon's glory in 1 Kings?

4. According to the text, from which nations did Solomon marry foreign women? For which gods did he build altars?

5. What three adversaries did the Lord raise up as punishment?

6. Which adversary was promised a portion of the kingdom of Israel?

QUESTIONS FOR DISCUSSION

1. Many of Solomon's acts in this lesson were spiritually ambiguous, but they eventually led to his downfall. How can the mindset, "Well, the Bible doesn't say it's wrong," sometimes hurt our spiritual walk?

2. Though Solomon's riches were a gift from God, they eventually helped to lead him astray. How can the blessing of prosperity lead us astray?

3. Do you think the church sometimes wrestles with materialistic attitudes? If so, how?

4. How can faithfulness to God be a challenge for the young? How can it be a challenge for the old? Is it harder to serve God in one's youth or in old age? Defend your answer.

5. Should Christians marry non-Christians? Why or why not?

6. What for you is the biggest takeaway from Solomon's life?

5

THE DIVIDED KINGDOM

1 KINGS 12-13

Objective: To understand why the kingdom
of Israel divided during Rehoboam's reign

INTRODUCTION

With Solomon asleep with his fathers, his son, Rehoboam, was poised to
inherit all of his father's glory. But things quickly went south when Israel
asked Rehoboam to ease their oppression. However, Solomon's son crude-
ly and caustically spurned their request, inciting schism and ill will that
would last decades. Despite virulent efforts at forced unification, Israel remained divided because such was God's will.

EXAMINATION

Read 1 Kings 12:1-24. As Israel's post-Solomonic history unfolds, it's easy
to conclude that the kingdom divided overnight. But Solomon's empire had
been a house of cards in many ways. His magnificent building programs,
which had brought Israel so much acclaim and pride, had been built on the
backs of forced laborers and financed by heavy taxes.

That said, Rehoboam certainly did himself no favors. He went to

Shechem to be made king, but the inauguration turned into an interrogation. A contingent, led by the just-returned-from-exile Jeroboam, beseeched the king to lighten up on the forced labor and high taxes. Rehoboam responded with something amounting to, "Let me check with my people and get back to you in three days."

When Rehoboam consulted his father's advisors, they unanimously counseled him to rule as a servant-leader (v. 7). This, they said, was the only way to forge national unity among the disparate tribes. But the advice of the king's younger advisors was decidedly worse. "Thus you should say to them, 'My little finger is thicker than my father's loins'" (v. 10 NRSV).

It must be remembered that "young" here is relative. Rehoboam was forty-one years old, and his friends were presumably about the same age. What is telling, however, is how closely Rehoboam identified with the younger vs. older advisors; note the use of *we* vs. *I* in v. 9, suggesting Rehoboam was predisposed to follow their counsel. In the thinking of these young advisors, the only way to forge national unity was by being a bully.

The Northern tribes' response to Rehoboam was predictable. "To your tents, O Israel!" amounted to a repudiation of the Davidic dynasty. "To your tents" had once functioned as an expression of release from military service (cf. 1 Sam 4:10; 2 Sam 20:22). But the saying had evolved as a proverb expressing dissatisfaction with the present administration, and we are left to wonder if ridding themselves of the house of David was what the Northern tribes had desired all along.

In an ill-advised attempt to settle the dispute by force, Rehoboam sent Adoram, who as a young man had been an official in David's cabinet (2 Sam. 20:24) and later served as Solomon's overseer of forced labor (4:6). In retrospect, Rehoboam couldn't have chosen a worse person for this mission. Adoram was stoned, and the king fled for his life. Like "the shot heard round the world" at Concord, Massachusetts in 1775, or the firing on Fort Sumter in 1861, Adoram's assassination signaled the beginning of hostilities. And though this would be mostly a cold war, things wouldn't thaw out for several decades.

In a last-ditch effort to keep the two factions united, Rehoboam mustered 180,000 troops from Judah and Benjamin to quell the rebellion. But on the eve of battle, the prophet Shemaiah brought Rehoboam a message from the Lord: the division was a divine decree. Rehoboam had no business resisting any longer. Go home and deal with it.

Read 1 Kings 12:25-33. Jeroboam's first order of business as king was to fortify his capital at Shechem, and he later did the same at Penuel. While Jeroboam's fortification endeavors were arguably spiritually neutral, it was his second order of business that left the narrator hotter than a hornet. In what was, at least in Jeroboam's mind, a politically expedient move necessary to solidify his rule, the king had alternative worship centers established at Dan and Bethel, each one complete with the image of a golden calf.

Dan and Bethel represented polar ends of the Northern Kingdom. Bethel lay on Ephraim's border with Benjamin, some eleven miles north of Jerusalem, and it was a traditional worship site dating to the time of Abraham and Jacob. Dan lay on Israel's northern boundary, and it too had a religious history (Judg. 18:27-31), but one considerably more dubious than Bethel. Thus, Bethel continued to be a prominent locale in the Northern Kingdom (Hos. 10:5; Amos 7:13); for one thing, Bethel benefited from a better location—Israelites making the trip to Jerusalem would find Bethel a more convenient destination.

Scholars are not in agreement as to what exactly these calves represented. Some believe Jeroboam never intended the calves to be an act of unfaithfulness to the covenant, and that the negative light in which Jeroboam is cast in this section is really just the fault of a grouchy narrator with a bone to pick. There are, however, several facts that blow holes in such an interpretation. *First, there is no question that we are to see in this calf story a reflection of the original golden calf story of Exodus 32.*

- Like Aaron (Exod. 32:2-4), Jeroboam oversaw the construction of the calves (v. 28).
- Like Aaron (Exod. 32:4), Jeroboam announced, "Behold your gods, O Israel, who brought you up out of the land of Egypt (v. 28).
- Like Aaron (Exod. 32:5), Jeroboam established a new altar and a new feast (vv. 32-33).

Second, the calves were too closely identifiable with the idolatry of Israel's neighbors. These calves would have been confusing at best and deceptive at worst. Those with an imperfect understanding of Israel's God, especially those who used to worship Baal, would have conflated these calves to be representative of God and not just his footstool.

Finally, what Jeroboam thought he was doing matters little. Whether he broke the first commandment or the second, the narrator is dismayed that Jeroboam violated any of them in the first place. Whether he is abandoning the worship of the true God, or simply perverting Israel's worship, the end result is the same.

But Jeroboam's apostasy was not limited to the calves. The narrator also records that he established alternate temples on high places at Dan and Bethel, installed non-Levitical priests, and instituted a new feast to rival the Feast of Booths, typically celebrated in the seventh month in Jerusalem. Each of these changes violated what God had clearly ordained in the Law of Moses.

Jeroboam was God's anointed for Israel and the bearer of divine blessing, but the promises of God were not enough for him. Jeroboam could not be convinced that the people of Israel truly supported him; they would surely assassinate him and defect to Judah if they went to worship at the Temple one too many times. Though he was king of ten tribes, he secretly considered Rehoboam to be his "lord" (v. 27).

All that was required to secure his kingdom was Jeroboam's obedience, but he could not give it. The prophetic word had encouraged him to do "as David my servant did" (11:38); instead, the actions he takes in vv. 28-33 all arise from doubt in the veracity of God's word.

Read 1 Kings 13. While Jeroboam was leading worship at Bethel, an anonymous prophet interrupted festivities. The prophet from Judah cried out against the altar. He spoke of a time three hundred years in the future when a king named Josiah, a descendant of David, would desecrate this altar (a taboo akin to burning the American flag) by burning human corpses upon it. To confirm that his message was indeed heaven-sent, a sign would accompany it: "Behold, the altar shall be torn down, and the ashes that are on it shall be poured out" (v. 3).

Jeroboam growled at the prophet and screamed, "Seize him!" But the words were scarcely out of his mouth when his hand "dried up, so that he could not draw it back to himself" (v. 4), perhaps a condition known today as cataplexy in which a shock to the nervous system causes muscle rigidity. Also, as the prophet had predicted, the altar "was ripped apart, and the ashes poured from the altar" (v. 5 HCSB), making both the altar and Jeroboam's sacrifice ritually unclean (cf. Lev 6:10-11) in much the same way that allowing the American flag to touch the ground disqualifies it from future service.

Justifiably panicked, Jeroboam pleaded with the nameless prophet to pray on his behalf so that his arm might be healed, and the prophet did so. God's miraculous healing further confirmed that all this was from the Lord (note that this is the third sign—a significant biblical number—to Jeroboam in the passage). No doubt grateful, the king invited this prophet to dine with him, but the prophet steadfastly refused.

It seems to us as arbitrary or inane that God would require the prophet to return home a different way than he came. The perceived inconvenience of doing so is compounded when we realize that a major highway ran from Jerusalem to Bethel, and to require the prophet to return home a different way meant he had to forgo the interstate for a washed-out dirt road. But in obedience to the divine word, the unnamed prophet did just that.

Meanwhile, an old prophet in Bethel (also unnamed) heard of what had happened when his sons "returned from church." After inquiring as to what direction the first prophet had taken, the old prophet of Bethel caught up on his donkey to the Judean man of God who was resting under an oak tree. When the Judean prophet was invited to the home of the Bethel prophet, he objected again, relating the divine command.

But then a twist—the old prophet informs his Southern counterpart that a new word of the Lord has gone out. "I am also a prophet, just like you. And an angel came to me with a message from GOD: 'Bring him home with you, and give him a good meal!'" (v. 18 Msg). So that we know the truth, however, the narrator informs us that the old prophet of Bethel was lying.

With false assurance, the Judean prophet trusted this new "word of the LORD" and returned with the old prophet to Bethel. But during their meal, the old prophet was suddenly seized by the Spirit with a prophetic word—a bona fide word from God, a message of judgment, and for the Judean prophet! He who had faithfully discharged his responsibility at first was now judged for failing to complete it. He would die on his way home and be denied dignity as to his final resting place.

Sure enough, as he returned to Judah, the formerly-faithful prophet was attacked by a lion. But lest we judge this to be simply a random accident, the narrator informs us that the lion stood guard over the body, but did not devour it, nor did it attack a perfectly delectable donkey. Passers-by were understandably struck by the odd scene, and news quickly reached the old prophet in Bethel.

No doubt profoundly saddened over his culpability, the old prophet of Bethel retrieved his colleague's body and buried him in his own family tomb. In addition, he charged his sons to bury him with the Judean prophet, choosing to identify with him in death, now realizing that the word of judgment spoken against Bethel (and all the Northern Kingdom) was a potent word that would surely come to pass.

APPLICATION

Groupthink. Though Rehoboam solicited the opinion of his older advisors, it's clear he did not identify with them as much as he did the younger (v. 9). Had Rehoboam remained more objective and encouraged vigorous, respectful debate on the issue, perhaps he would have made a wiser decision. In families, churches, and businesses, there can be intense pressure to conform to "keep the peace" and not "rock the boat." But at times, this only means we are expected to submit to stronger alpha personalities and allow them to have their way. Perhaps all of us would benefit if we remembered Paul's command when it came to interpersonal relationships (Eph. 5:21). Effective leaders do not perceive dissent as a threat. Rather, they (at the least) consider it an opportunity to affirm the dissenter's value to the group and (at the most) welcome it as a chance to discern flaws in their plan. Healthy disagreement today can spare us many headaches tomorrow.

God's Sovereignty. Whenever this story is told, emphasis is almost always placed on Rehoboam's foolishness in listening to the wrong advisors. But such was only one of many threads in the grand tapestry of Israel's dissolution. Ultimately, Israel divided because it was God's will that she do so. This section of Kings is ripe with examples of the potency of God's will and Word. He will either work through us or in spite of us, but he will see his will done on earth as it is in heaven. This gives Christians hope that the foolishness and sinfulness of men cannot ultimately triumph; God is in charge. Our duty is to faithfully do God's will and leave the consequences to him. If kingdoms split apart, let it be because of someone else's foolishness, not ours. Let God look down and find us trusting and obeying him in all things.

Faithful in Small Things. Early in the story of 1 Kings 13, we are impressed with the Judean prophet's boldness. His is a fortitude every Christian should aspire to. But while he in one moment was faithful while under threat, he let his guard down in another over something as "trivial" as which way to go home and whether to do so directly. Likewise, some Christians are bold enough to rise to the occasion in "big moments," but they lack the wisdom and fortitude to take on smaller, more nuanced challenges. As one writer puts it, "We can muster defiance for the danger of the hour but cannot find discernment for the ploy of the moment." Let us not prove faithful in large things, but lax in small ones. Let us be deliberate as to the path we take and the direction we turn—such could be a matter of life and death.

CONCLUSION

Before we know it, Israel's glory years faded into oblivion, and the nation was divided in two. On the surface, the division seemed to be the product of Rehoboam's foolishness and Jeroboam's instigation. But God was working behind the scenes. This gives Christians hope that, whether we face good times or bad, success or failure, blessings or hardships, we know God is in control. The only proper response is to trust and obey God in all things, confident that he will care for us. We can only control what we can control.

QUESTIONS FOR REFLECTION

1. Which group of advisors was Rehoboam more predisposed to identify and agree with? Why?

2. Whom did Rehoboam select to try and force the tribes to reunite? Why was this choice such a bad idea?

3. When he mustered troops for civil war, who told Rehoboam to return home and accept the division?

4. What changes did Jeroboam introduce to the Northern Kingdom?

5. What commandments did Jeroboam violate with his changes?

6. Why was the anonymous prophet commanded to return home without delay?

7. When the prophet of Bethel invited the Judean prophet home for a meal, why did the Judean prophet follow him?

QUESTIONS FOR DISCUSSION

1. In what ways have you seen families, churches, or businesses stifle healthy disagreement? How can leaders encourage healthy dissent?

2. How can we discern healthy disagreement from unhealthy dissension? How can we tell if someone is warning of trouble vs. being a trouble-maker?

3. How have you seen God use division to accomplish his will?

4. Jeroboam introduced changes to Israel's worship, and it eventually cost him his kingdom. What cautionary tale does this provide the church?

5. Read Gal. 1:9; Heb. 1:1-2. Like the Judean prophet, are we sometimes guilty of listening to "another message from God" instead of the original? If so, how?

6. Like the Judean prophet, in what ways do you think the church is bold in the "big moments" but weak in the face of subtle, smaller challenges?

6

FROM BAD TO WORSE

1 KINGS 14-16

Objective: To observe how spiritual
unfaithfulness can lead to national instability

INTRODUCTION

Every sports fan has witnessed the spectacular collapse—the agonizing occasion when their favorite team snatches defeat from the jaws of victory.
Whereas we once thought victory certain, loss occurs, and we are left to
marvel, "Wow, that escalated quickly!"

That same feeling begins to settle in as we study 1 Kings 14-16. Not
too far removed from the account of Solomon's glory, we witness both Israel and Judah descend into political and spiritual chaos. The Northern
Kingdom especially goes from bad to worse in this section, and primarily
because of her idolatry. The corporate consequences of disobedience become quite conspicuous.

EXAMINATION

Read 1 Kings 14:1-20. Not long after the prophet had denounced the altar at
Bethel, Jeroboam's son, Abijah, became gravely ill. It was not uncommon in

ancient times for a seer of some sort to be consulted on whether full health would be recovered. Jeroboam had a lot of confidence in the prophet Ahijah since the latter had prophesied that Jeroboam would be king in the first place (11:29-39). Long ago, Ahijah had told Jeroboam that his rule would be established by God. But Jeroboam had failed to trust and obey, so now, feeble Ahijah had the difficult task of making known the fate of the royal family.

The prophetic word began with a biting indictment of Jeroboam's sins. God had exalted him as leader, but instead of becoming a king in David's footsteps, Jeroboam had incited the wrath of heaven by his idolatry. Because he had effectively cast the Lord behind his back, Jeroboam's dynasty would be treated similarly.

The judgment was not just for Jeroboam, but for "every male" of his house. This phrase, however, is just a nicer way of expressing what the Hebrew literally says—"he who urinates against a wall" (cf. KJV). There is an intentional link between urine and dung in v. 10, and we must allow this divine vulgarity to underscore the gravity of Jeroboam's wickedness.

Jeroboam's punishment was not limited to himself and his house, but the entire Northern Kingdom. The Lord would "strike Israel as a reed is shaken in the water, and root up Israel out of this good land that he gave to their fathers and scatter them beyond the Euphrates" (v. 15). Indeed, the history of the Northern Kingdom would be one of instability ("a rattled reed") and ultimate exile ("rooted up") from which she'd never return.

Jeroboam's wife returned to Tirzah (seven miles northeast of Shechem) with a mother's broken heart. The nation mourned and buried Abijah, and the word of the Lord was fulfilled, for it stands forever. After more than two decades of rule, Jeroboam himself died and was buried. A ruler with so much promise, one handpicked by God as Saul had been, reigned in folly because he cared too much about popular opinion and not enough about heaven's.

Read 1 Kings 14:21-31. During Rehoboam's reign, Judah was not faithful to the Lord, but rather provoked him as Jeroboam did with his idolatry. The influence of Israel's pagan neighbors had begun under Solomon and is invoked by the narrator with mention of Rehoboam's mother (Naamah the Ammonite). Like the nations around them, and the Canaanites before them, Israel established high places, pillars, Asherim, and cult prostitution as a part of their worship (vv. 23-24). The Lord had demanded that these be banished (Exod. 34:13; Deut. 12:3; 23:17-18), but they were not.

As punishment for Rehoboam's faithlessness, God sent the scourge of

Pharaoh Shishak against Jerusalem. Shishak looted the Temple, the palace, and terrorized the surrounding countryside (including the Northern Kingdom). The narrator uses the occasion to offer up an anecdote concerning the erosion of Solomon's glory in Israel. Whereas he had had shields of gold for his guards, these were carried off by Shishak as spoil, and Rehoboam could only afford replacements of bronze. Worse, so paranoid was he of losing them that he kept them under lock and key when not used for ceremonial purposes. We obviously have come a long way since Solomon's day when silver was as common as rocks (10:27).

Notice of Rehoboam's reign ends with the standard formula in which the narrator directs the reader to other sources, then notes the king's burial and successor. He also reminds us that there was war (or more precisely, a general spirit of hostility) between Rehoboam and Jeroboam throughout their reigns.

Read 1 Kings 15:1-8. Like Rehoboam, his father, Abijam was wicked, since "his heart was not wholly true to the LORD his God." As will become standard for Judah's kings, his righteousness is compared with that of David. But unexpectedly, the narrator tells us that God is faithful to the Davidic dynasty for David's sake and in spite of Abijam's evil. It is for that reason that God maintains a lamp for David in Jerusalem. In the Old Testament, *lamp* is symbolic of one's posterity. Though a man may be dead and gone, his life and work were not "extinguished" if he had descendants in the land of the living.

Twice in his closing comments on Abijam, the narrator speaks of war with the Northern tribes (vv. 6-7). The double mention might be intended to stress that this is not just Abijam's war, but one he inherited from his father. In fact, the chapter mentions "war" four times (vv. 6, 7, 16, 32), highlighting how it was an ongoing struggle.

Read 1 Kings 15:9-24. While Asa reigned forty-one years on Judah's throne, the throne of Israel saw six different monarchs. At the beginning, Asa's grandmother, Maacah, remained in the position of queen mother. But he soon deposed her "because she had made an abominable image for Asherah" (v. 13).

Though the narrator's comments on Asa are not totally positive—he didn't remove the high places—it's true that he was Judah's best king since at least Solomon and possibly David. Unlike his father, "the heart of Asa was wholly true to the LORD all his days" (v. 14; cf. v. 3). In fact, the narrator of Kings gives greater honor only to Hezekiah and Josiah. Asa expelled the cult prostitutes, tore down the idols of his predecessors, ousted Maacah from her position of influence, and burned the queen mother's Asherah image in the Kidron. Asa also restored some of the Temple's treasures.

Despite Asa's faithfulness, he did not enjoy the peace Solomon had—"there was war between Asa and Baasha king of Israel all their days" (v. 16). Baasha, the Northern king, antagonized Judah by fortifying Ramah. Located 5½ miles north of Jerusalem, Ramah was a Benjaminite city on the border of Ephraim that lay at the intersection of two important military/economic routes. By fortifying that city, Baasha essentially pigeon-holed Asa in Jerusalem without a means of escape (v. 17).

In retaliation, Asa solicited the help of the Syrian king, Ben-hadad. Chronicles explicitly condemns Asa's appealing for help to a Gentile instead of the Lord (2 Chron. 16:7-10), but Kings is more subtle in its criticism. Asa took the Temple treasures previously donated (v. 15) and offered them to Ben-hadad as a "present" (v. 19)—the Hebrew word translated "present" elsewhere means "bribe" (e.g., Deut. 27:25; Psa. 26:10; Ezek. 22:12). Why did a righteous son of David appeal to a Gentile in his war against a fellow Israelite instead of trust God?

To get Baasha off Asa's back, Ben-hadad attacked and conquered four locations in northern Israel. Baasha was forced to abandon his building program at Ramah and redirect resources to ward off the threat. With this move, the Syrians solidified a foothold in the Northern Kingdom and would remain an antagonist for the next two centuries.

Meanwhile, Asa seized the building materials at Ramah and used them to fortify Geba and Mizpah. Asa was intent on creating a decent buffer between Judah and Israel so that Jerusalem could not be blockaded quite so easily in the future. Asa's biography ends with a note that "he was diseased in his feet" towards the end of his life (v. 23), and diagnosis has ranged from from gout to venereal disease.

Read 1 Kings 15:25-32. Following Asa's death, we are introduced to the reign of Nadab, Jeroboam's heir. Nadab was a case of "like father, like son"—a common theme among the Northern kings. Because of his wickedness, he only served something over twelve months in 909-908.

In 908, Israel laid siege to the Philistine town Gibbethon, located a dozen miles from the Mediterranean coast. Gibbethon was a strategic border town on the western edge of the hills of Judah. During the siege, Nadab was assassinated by Baasha of Issachar (likely a military commander), and the rest of Jeroboam's family was summarily exterminated, fulfilling Ahijah's prophecy (14:10-11).

With Nadab's assassination, a lengthy period of instability commences in Israel. Six different men would reign over the Northern Kingdom in less than thirty years as opposed to just one in Judah during the same period. We cannot help but wonder if the extreme internal instability that came to characterize the Northern Kingdom was a result of God's judgment on her wickedness.

Read 1 Kings 15:33-16:7. Nadab's assassin, Baasha, set up his capital at Tirzah and reigned for 24 years. He is the first of several Northern kings to seize power via assassination. Any hopes of spiritual reform are immediately dashed. Like his predecessors, he was wicked in the Lord's eyes and copied Jeroboam's apostasy.

A prophet, Jehu son of Hanani, brought a message of judgment. Like Jeroboam, Baasha had been hand-picked by God and "exalted [...] out of the dust" to the throne. The word translated "ruler" is indicative of one divinely appointed to rule or lead, and was used of David (1 Sam. 25:30), Jeroboam (1 Kgs. 14:7), and Hezekiah (2 Kgs. 20:5). It is not very different from the concept of *messiah*.

But despite being the Lord's anointed, Baasha responded by perpetuating spiritual rebellion, and the people only continued in "provoking [God] to anger with their sins" (v. 2). Thus, God's wrath would be poured out on the house of Baasha as it had on Jeroboam. Baasha's destiny was the worst imaginable by someone in the ancient world. But the divine warning seems to have had no effect on him.

Read 1 Kings 16:8-20. Baasha's son, Elah, reigned just a few months during two different years. The context of his demise may signal something to us about Elah's weakness or indulgence. While the king was enjoying a red Solo cup party, Zimri dispatched Elah. Though Zimri likely eliminated Elah's entire family so as to minimize the chances of any kinfolk seeking blood vengeance, his thoroughness unwittingly fulfilled God's word spoken through his prophet, Jehu. The dedication of the family of Baasha to idols brought them only destruction and death.

In what has to be one of history's shortest regencies, the assassin Zimri reigned a whopping seven days. After learning of Elah's assassination, Omri abandoned the siege against the Philistines at Gibbethon and hurried some forty miles north to Tirzah, the capital. Omri quickly took control of the city, at which point Zimri set fire to the palace, choosing death by conflagration over execution by Omri.

Read 1 Kings 16:21-28. When Zimri's week-long reign went up in flames, the Northern Kingdom descended into civil war. On one side was "Tibni the son of Ginath," and on the other was Omri. After a four-year struggle (cf. vv. 15, 23), somehow Omri seized the throne. He was Israel's sixth king in less than fifty years.

We are never told why Omri decided to relocate the capital from Tirzah twelve miles west to Samaria, but the new site had much to commend it. It was certainly a more advantageous location, both politically and militarily—the city sat on a hill three hundred feet higher in elevation than the surrounding plain and was eminently defensible. It also offered better economic opportunities since it was connected to major trade routes to the north, west, and south. In exchange for the site, Omri paid Shemer a premium of 150 pounds of silver (worth about $15-20 million today) for roughly 160 acres of real estate.

In every way imaginable, Omri is the first strong king of Israel since (and is arguably superior to) Jeroboam. He strengthened the military, stabilized the economy, and made great strides in international relations. None of that matters, however, in divine history. All the narrator is interested in is Omri's faithfulness to God and the Law, of which there was none. In fact, he is notorious for doing "more evil than all who were before him" (v. 25). Like Jeroboam and Baasha, Omri received from God a chance for a fresh start in Israel, but when it came to idolatry, it was just business as usual.

Read 1 Kings 16:29-34. If Omri was bad, Ahab was worse. Ahab married Jezebel, the princess of Tyre and Sidon. As with Solomon, Ahab's choice of spouse became a corrupting influence in Israel. Upon her nuptials, Jezebel introduced her patron god to both her husband and her adopted country. Whereas there once had been only an altar and calf in Bethel and Dan, there is now a temple of Baal and an Asherah pole in Samaria.

Like his father, historians remember Ahab as a gifted ruler and formidable military opponent. In 853, a significant international alliance opposed the Assyrian ruler Shalmaneser III at the battle of Qarqar, and Ahab is noted for his significant contributions to the fray. Closer to home, Ahab established peace with the Philistines and maintained control of Moab across the Jordan.

But to the narrator, worldly greatness paled in comparison to spiritual fidelity to the first two commandments. It seems a leader can establish a strong national defense, a vibrant economy, and enjoy massive popularity among the masses, yet still be a complete failure in God's eyes.

APPLICATION

Jeroboam's Son. The most repugnant part of this section is the death of Abijah, Jeroboam's son. We understand why Jeroboam must be punished, but why must his son have to die? And to compound matters, why is Abijah's death *because* of his virtue (v. 13)? For whatever reason, it was God's will in the Old Testament "that the sins of the parents may be visited upon the children and the grandchildren, to the third and fourth generation 'of those who reject me'" (Exod. 20:5). Though this is no longer true today in a strict sense (cf. Ezek. 18:21), it remains true that our disobedience sometimes negatively impacts not just ourselves and our families, but the entire community. This, in fact, will become the enduring legacy of Jeroboam.

David's Lamp. Conspicuously missing from the account of Rehoboam's and Abijam's reign is a prophecy predicting doom because of their disobedience. God's commitment to the house of David was strong, and he graciously showed David's descendants greater patience than the kings of the North. Throughout Kings, this concept is often referred to as the "lamp of David." In the same way, while our sins often cost others, God also shows us grace because of Christ. In Romans, Paul celebrates the fact that those in Christ are exempt from condemnation (Rom. 8:1). Just as David's dynasty received unmerited favor because of David, so we receive unmerited favor because of Jesus.

Kicking the Can. With Asa, there begins a troubling trend in Judah that will hasten her downfall. With the exception of Hezekiah and Josiah, the righteous rulers of the Southern Kingdom always failed to root out the idolatrous high places. Though some were personally opposed to idolatry, it was not their policy to exterminate pagan worship from the suburbs surrounding Jerusalem. Content they must have been to kick the can down the road, hoping the issue would take care of itself at some later date. But the thing is, such issues almost never go away on their own. Instead, they fester, rot, and lead to the decay of the community. Sin, like cancer, doesn't go away on its own. It must be rudely and ruthlessly rooted out if we are ever to be healthy again (cf. 1 Cor. 5; Heb. 3:12-13).

CONCLUSION

After burning through several kings, the Northern Kingdom stabilizes during the reigns of Omri and Ahab. But this is a false stability, for though they are effective leaders from a secular standpoint, they are abject failures in a spiritual sense. Indeed, Israel's stability during this period is due solely to the Lord's goodness, proof that he does not always immediately abandon his people at the first sign of sin.

In the chapters that follow, God brings a lot of judgment on Israel: men of God step forward with somber warnings of judgment. Rain is withheld for three years. Israel's enemies at times gain the upper hand against her. But it is always for a reason: God is seeking to reclaim Israel. In what follows, we are reminded that acts of God's judgment are also acts of grace.

QUESTIONS FOR REFLECTION

1. Why was Jeroboam and his dynasty condemned to death? Why was Jeroboam's downfall predicted in such graphic terms?

2. How is Solomon's fading glory illustrated in Shishak's attack of Jerusalem?

3. Though he was quick to judge and destroy rulers of the Northern Kingdom, why was God reluctant to wipe out the families of the kings in Jerusalem?

4. Rather than trust God for deliverance, what did Asa do to meet the threat posed by Baasha?

5. Between Jeroboam's death and Ahab's accession (a period of about thirty-five years), how many kings ruled over the Northern Kingdom? List them.

6. How many different capital cities did the Northern Kingdom have during this period? Name them.

QUESTIONS FOR DISCUSSION

1. In Kings, God often destroyed an entire family because of the father's disobedience. Does God do so today? What does the New Testament say about this?

2. Sometimes others suffer because of our sin. How have you seen this principle illustrated in your life?

3. Specifically, how have you seen sin and unfaithfulness lead to corporate instability?

4. Just as the kings of Judah were shown greater patience because of David, God shows us greater patience because of Christ. Is this a license to sin? If not, why not?

5. Have you known leaders who swept thorny issues under the rug, hoping the issue would go away on its own? Was that strategy successful? Explain.

6. How is sin like a cancer? Why must it ruthlessly rooted out?

7

ELIJAH VS. BAAL

1 KINGS 17

Objective: To reaffirm that God alone
knows how to take care of his people

INTRODUCTION

Elijah is truly one of the most remarkable figures in the Old Testament.
He casts an impressive shadow across the history of Israel. In this opening chapter, we see the care that God provided for this prophet; in every
way, he was God's man of the hour, the prophet tapped to stand up to the
unprecedented wickedness of Ahab and Jezebel. Through Elijah, a faithful
God continued to demonstrate his concern to a faithless people.

EXAMINATION

Read 1 Kings 17:1-7. In his debut on the stage of Scripture, Elijah could
not have been more uncouth had he tried. Elijah showed up to declare a
ban on rain until he said so. And then, just as suddenly and mysteriously as
he had entered the scene, Elijah disappeared.

Ahab would have considered Elijah's prediction of drought to be a
threat to the throne. In ancient times, kings were responsible for adequate

rainfall like presidents are responsible for national economies.

Elijah's message would have also been threatening to Baal worship. In the worldview of Ahab and Jezebel, Baal sent dew in the summer and rain in the winter to nourish the earth since he was the god of fertility. Servants of Baal sought his favor in exchange for plenteous crops, fertile wombs for women and livestock, and anything else they desired to prosper and multiply.

Considering that virtually 100% of ancient Israel's economy was directly dependent on agriculture, the threat of drought was especially grave. In the worst way imaginable, Elijah's declaration made him persona non grata. Later, we're told Ahab had been searching for Elijah while the latter had been AWOL, probably thinking that getting rid of the prophet would end the drought since Elijah was "the cause."

The prophet's prediction now delivered, God commanded Elijah to depart for a stream called Cherith in Transjordan. There, Elijah was sustained by God with water from the brook and food brought to him by ravens. As long as I've known this story, I've imagined Elijah subsisting on meager rations, not unlike the Israelites living off of manna in the wilderness. The mental picture left me quite sympathetic of Elijah. "Poor guy," I thought. "There couldn't have been much joy in his meals—it was for the birds!"

However, Elijah lived in a time when only the wealthy could afford to have meat as a part of their regular diet. The narrator, then, by telling us that the ravens brought bread and meat to Elijah, intends for us to see this exiled prophet feasting like a king while the rest of Israel suffered during the drought and resulting famine. And while many might have been lucky to have one substantive meal each day, Elijah was feasting morning and night. And one scholar reminds us that brooks and streams (i.e., wadis) in that part of the world were seasonal, meaning they ran dry when the rain ceased and even pools would not have survived a drought. But Cherith yielded water for Elijah for a long time. Unlike Baal, God knows how to take care of those faithful to him!

But things weren't this way forever. Eventually, the brook dried up, and Elijah was called away by God yet again. Elijah could have sat by Cherith and pouted about the loss of water and food. Why had God stopped providing? Had he been defeated by Baal? Or, worse, was God's withdrawal of provision a sign of his displeasure with Elijah?

Read 1 Kings 17:8-16. With Cherith now a dry stream bed, the Lord commanded Elijah to go to Zarephath, a Phoenician town located eight miles south of Sidon and eighty miles north of Samaria. The irony of this location is that it, like Cherith, was beyond the domain of Ahab, but was also in Jezebel's backyard and thus on Baal's home turf.

If I had been Elijah, it would have been more than a little disconcerting to hear God say, "Go to this place because I've arranged for a widow to take care of you there." Widows in ancient times were often destitute. So when Elijah was told about the circumstances of his new benefactor, it couldn't have been faith-inspiring.

When Elijah came upon this widow, the narrator says she was "gathering sticks," and I think we are to imagine her hunched over at the city gate, scrounging for random branches for a fire. A lot of traffic would have passed through the gate each day, and people would have dropped things. Whether intentionally or coincidentally, the narrator's depiction of this widow reminds us of another widow, Ruth, who stumbled upon God's providence while also foraging for a meager meal.

The widow's plight is illustrated by Elijah requesting a morsel of bread, only for the widow to respond that she has none, that she is indeed preparing for herself and her son a last supper of sorts. She is at the end of her rope, but Elijah speaks to her fear by reasserting his request for bread. Though she has but only a handful of flour and a little oil, her meager gift—when coupled with faith—will bring a bountiful return. Elijah brought a word from the Lord, an assurance that her flour and oil would not run out, and God's word came to pass. Even in enemy territory, the Lord proved himself quite capable of caring for those whom Baal had forgotten.

Read 1 Kings 17:17-24. So far, the Lord has soundly proven his superiority to Baal in Israel and Phoenicia. He can provide for his prophet and for the poor when they have nothing. Baal is no match for the Lord's providence. But there remains one last lingering question: What of death?

Sometime later, the Zarephath widow's son became sick and died. Any woman who lost her husband in ancient times was placed in a difficult circumstance, but those without children faced a particularly grim future. So we should empathize with her as she believes her world to be crashing down around her. There is pain and bitterness and incredulity in her voice when she said to Elijah, "Why did you ever show up here in the first place—a holy man barging in, exposing my sins, and killing my son?" (v. 18 Msg).

Elijah carried the widow's deceased son to the upstairs room the prophet had been occupying during his time in Zarephath. He laid the child out on the bed and then "stretched himself upon the child three times." In a very tender moment of painful honesty, the prophet pleaded with God to restore life to the boy, and "the LORD listened."

What had been dead was now alive by Elijah's petition and God's power. Baal had been powerless to end the drought; he had also been powerless to return a son to his mother. God did what Baal could not. How joyful the widow must have been to receive her son back to life! The miracle confirmed for her that Elijah was who he said he was, and that the Lord indeed would do all he had promised.

APPLICATION

Blessings in Disguise. When God removes a blessing, we too often chalk it up to divine impotence or dissatisfaction. First, God is anything but powerless. The Bible repeatedly reiterates that nothing is impossible for him. But second, though he might be displeased with us at times, a dried-up stream can just as easily mean that the Lord has greater work for us to do. In other words, what we interpret as divine displeasure could also be God saying that it's time to move on, that there is more work to be done. On the other hand, comfort and ease often insulate us from assuming the risk of obedience to the divine call.

For the Birds. It is not insignificant God's provision is so immense in this passage, especially on Elijah's behalf. That Elijah ate meat, and twice a day while at Cherith is remarkable. Despite what circumstances may indicate at times, those in Christ are never truly in need, for God supplies. And compared to what would be possible left to ourselves, God always supplies in abundance. A bird in God's hand is worth two in our own bush; a day in his courts are worth a thousand elsewhere. God's provision is always greater than what we could find anywhere else.

Spiritual Amnesia. The widow's complaint to Elijah in v. 18 is understandable. She assumed that her obedience and hospitality to the prophet would have insulated her from tragedy. She now concludes that her son's death is punishment for some sin, that she somehow deserves this. And though she blamed Elijah for her son's death, she forgets that she and her son would both be dead at this point were it not for the prophet. Most everyone is tempted to blame God for our problems, but doing so only blinds us to his providence. Remembering God's past faithfulness helps sustain us until his future provision becomes a reality.

CONCLUSION

Unlike Baal, God knows how to take care of those faithful to him. He proved greater than Baal by sending a drought, yet providing for Elijah. He proved greater than Baal in Baal's own territory by providing for the widow. And he proved greater than Baal in raising a boy back to life. It may be that we are appointed in the will of God to suffer, to starve, or even to die. But we know that God will never forsake us; that he will supply for our every need in Christ (Phil. 4:19). In turn, we should seek opportunities to magnify the Lord in our suffering and so confirm his Word to the lost.

QUESTIONS FOR REFLECTION

1. How did Elijah's declaration in v. 1 pose both a political and religious threat to Ahab?

2. How was the drought proof of God's power over Baal?

3. Name the ways God provided for Elijah in this chapter.

4. What was the Zaraphath widow doing when Elijah arrived?

5. How was the miraculous provision for the widow proof of God's power over Baal?

6. What complaint did the widow make to Elijah when her son died?

7. How was raising the widow's son proof of God's power over Baal?

QUESTIONS FOR DISCUSSION

1. Has God ever lavishly provided for you while others were going through "lean" times? How so?

2. Have you ever interpreted the removal of God's blessing as a sign of God's displeasure? What was that like? Like Elijah, did you come to see it as a summons to greater work in service to God? If so, how?

3. How can comfort and ease keep us from serving the Lord as faithfully as we should?

4. How have you seen God's provision prove greater than your own?

5. Is it always true that our suffering is because we have done something wrong?

6. Have you, like the widow, ever been guilty of spiritual amnesia? If so, how?

8

ELIJAH VS. AHAB

1 KINGS 18

Objective: To celebrate God's supremacy
and power over all false gods

INTRODUCTION

In every way, Elijah was the man for Israel's hour. When faithfulness to the
Lord was at an all-time low, a prophet with true grit emerged from virtually nowhere. Grizzled, caustic, determined—these are the classic traits that
have become synonymous with Elijah. He was a man's man and a prophet's
prophet. In 1 Kings 18, he faced down Ahab and the false prophets of Baal
in one of Scripture's most dramatic scenes.

EXAMINATION

Read 1 Kings 18:1-19. After nearly three years of drought, it was time for
Elijah to confront Ahab and Jezebel once again. At God's direction, Elijah
emerged from hiding. Ironically, he had been under Ahab's nose the entire
time. Throughout this passage, God's power will be juxtaposed with Baal's
impotence.

We are introduced to a righteous servant of God named Obadiah.

Though he served as the administrator of Ahab's palace, "Obadiah feared the LORD greatly" (v. 3). At considerable risk to himself, he secreted away a hundred prophets—their opposition to Ahab and Jezebel being as much political as it was religious—in various caves in Israel and kept them alive with small rations of bread and water.

Ahab sent Obadiah out on a mission to find water and grass for his horses and mules. While searching, Obadiah stumbled upon the prophet and fell on his face in disbelief. Elijah bid him to bring Ahab to him, but Obadiah believed that to be a death wish. Ahab had left no stone unturned in his pursuit of Elijah—"There is no nation or kingdom where my lord has not sent to seek you. And when they would say, 'He is not here,' he would take an oath of the kingdom or nation, that they had not found you" (v. 10). So talented had Elijah been at hide-and-seek that Obadiah fully expected the prophet to disappear once again as soon as he had fetched the king, and then there would be no more Obadiah. But Elijah gave his word that such would not happen, and Obadiah did as he was told.

When Ahab laid eyes on the prophet, he greeted him by calling Elijah the "troubler of Israel." In the deluded mind of Israel's king, Elijah was solely to blame for the dire situation in which Israel found herself. Just as Achan had once brought trouble (and almost ruin) on Israel (Josh. 6:18; 7:25; cf. Saul, 1 Sam. 14:29) and had to be eliminated for the good of the community, so Ahab believed Elijah's life must be snuffed out if the drought was to abate.

But Ahab's sin had blinded him to the fact that he, not Elijah, was the Achan in this particular story, and Elijah says as much (v. 18). For his part, Elijah had had enough of Ahab's slander. To expose the king's god as a fraud, the prophet challenged Ahab and the false prophets of Baal and Asherah, those held in such high esteem by the queen of Israel, to meet him for the greatest contest of all time. The conflict at Carmel would prove to be one of the most dramatic scenes in Scripture.

Read 1 Kings 18:20-46. Located in northwestern Israel, Mount Carmel was considered sacred; it was the site of an ancient altar to Israel's God and also, at this point, a shrine to Baal. It was here that a lone prophet of the Lord and a multitude of prophets of Baal faced off against one another.

Elijah's initial question to his audience was, "How long will you go limping between two different opinions?" (v. 21). The verb translated "limping" is used only two other times in Scripture (v. 26; 2 Sam. 4:4).

Literally, Elijah was asking, "How long will you hobble on two crutches?" The nation of Israel was sick and lame, torn in two directions—Baal vs. the Lord—and was attempting to rely on both of them. The people's silent response to Elijah's question amounted to a concession that the prophet was right, so Elijah sought to settle everything once and for all.

The prophet's proposal called for two altars, two bulls, two sacrifices, but no fire. With everything prepared, each group would call on Baal or the Lord respectively, requesting that their altars be kindled with divine fire. The storm god of Canaan had to have a few lightning bolts laying around that could be spared for his dedicated servants—he was, after all, thought by the ancients to be the god in control of fire and lightning. But no fire would be coming from Baal. Elijah derided their pathetic attempts to start the fire (v. 27).

Eventually, Elijah had experienced enough amusement, and so he called the people to come closer, lest they think he had fooled them with sleight of hand. They repaired the traditional altar of the Lord on Carmel, one that had fallen into disrepair in recent times under Ahab and Jezebel's watch. The prophet took twelve stones to remake the altar and dug a trench large enough to hold 3½ gallons of water. With the sacrifice arranged, Elijah then requested that twelve jars of water be poured over all of it. Everything was soaked; the excess water filled the trench around the altar.

With that, the prophet turned his eyes to heaven and prayed. He invoked the names of the patriarchs, a reminder (not so much to God as to those present at Caramel) that Israel had a history with this God. He called upon the Lord to act so as to make himself known to Israel, to validate the prophet's deeds, and to turn his people back to the Lord. Desiring that God would make himself known and thereby reclaim the lost is among the noblest prayers we can offer.

In response to the gritty prophet's prayer, the fire of the Lord (commonly presumed to have been a lightning bolt, which would have amounted to beating Baal at his own game) descended in dramatic fashion and consumed everything: "the burnt offering and the wood and the stones and the dust, and licked up the water that was in the trench" (v. 38). So all-consuming was this fire from heaven that not even the altar survived. As one scholar concludes, "What seems at first to be a battle between two competing gods turns out instead to be a contest between God and an empty delusion."

After the roar from heaven, the people fell to the ground, confessing the Lord as the only God. Elijah ordered the execution of the false prophets; such bloodshed may offend our twenty-first-century sensibilities, but it served two purposes. First, Jezebel's slaughter of God's prophets (vv. 4, 13) had to be avenged. Second, Elijah was leading Israel in a recommitment to the covenant, one that demanded the execution of all false prophets (Deut. 13:1-5).

With such an impressive display of divine sovereignty, the Lord was now ready to restore rain to Israel. Elijah went up near the summit of Carmel and assumed a prone position with his head between his knees. In this posture, he prayed fervently (Jas. 5:18) that God would end the drought and send rain to Israel. He then instructed his servant to climb the summit seven times and report back as to what he saw. The first six times? Nothing. On the seventh? A cloud, but no larger than a man's fist.

And just like that, where there had just been a cloudless sky, the heavens quickly darkened "with clouds and wind, and there was a great rain" (v. 45). This wasn't a light afternoon shower—I like to imagine that what descended on Israel was what we would call in the South a "gully washer." And with this sudden torrent, God's victory over Baal is made complete.

APPLICATION

Unsung Hero. Obadiah's faithfulness to the Lord and the Lord's prophets must not be discounted. He is one of countless individuals who play very minor supporting roles in the biblical epic, yet whose faithfulness played no small part in the advancement of God's purposes in the world. His fear is understandable—he claims three times Ahab will kill him (vv. 9, 12, 14). But he is faithful nonetheless. For every great hero of faith, like Elijah, there are countless Obadiahs who serve in obscurity and behind the scenes. However, though they may never receive much adulation or appreciation from the world (or the church, for that matter), their dedication and strength does not go unnoticed by the Lord.

Baal vs. God. To non-Christians, the theme of Baal vs. God and Elijah's insistence that Israel choose (v. 21) can seem strange. We live in a country where the ability to choose one's own religion is a cherished liberty, and for good reason. But in a fallen world, religious freedom also brings with it the rise of tolerance, and a perverted definition of tolerance at that. Some have gone so far has to claim that religion (and the inherently exclusive claims of religion) has no place in the real world. It is imperative, then, that Christians confess—in word and deed—that one's religious convictions matter a great deal, and that those convictions ought to inform and pervade every arena of life, for our God pervades every sphere of life. In a culture where God has been banished to the hidden corners of life, we must become walking testimonies to the fact that all of life begins, is sustained by, and ultimately returns to God (Rom. 11:36).

The Silence of Idolatry. The failure of Baal to respond to his prophets offers a damning indictment on idolatry. False gods, whether ancient or modern, fail miserably to deliver or redeem us when such is most needed. There is no voice. There is no answer. No one pays us any attention. The idol of politics and government will always leave us feeling forsaken and ignored. The idol of materialism will always leave us feeling forsaken and ignored. Relationships. Health. Pleasure. Work. Anything or anyone that becomes our ultimate passion and pursuit will leave us empty, unless that One is he who has loved us since before the foundation of the world. When our despair is deep and need is great, we'll cry out for aid, but there will be no voice, no answer. No one will pay attention.

CONCLUSION

The chapter ends with one of Scripture's oddest scenes—the sight of Elijah outrunning Ahab's chariot down the slippery, muddy slopes of Carmel and on to Jezreel. Peter Leithart explains, "A runner before a king is a herald and a king's servant, and Elijah returns to Jezreel to announce that the blessing of [the Lord] has returned to the land and to proclaim the return of the king to one of his chief cities." For now, Ahab has committed himself to the Lord (not Baal) as God. But this wouldn't last for long—Jezebel would have something to say about Ahab's new religion, and she would turn the tables on Elijah.

QUESTIONS FOR REFLECTION

1. Though a servant of Ahab, what had Obadiah done to serve the Lord?

2. Why was Obadiah reluctant to leave Elijah and summon Ahab?

3. What did Ahab call Elijah upon laying eyes on the prophet?

4. List all of the ways the Lord proved superior to Baal in this chapter.

5. What did Elijah mention in his prayer before the altar?

6. What was the people's reaction to God consuming the altar?

7. Why did Elijah run before Ahab's chariot? What symbolic meaning did this have?

QUESTIONS FOR DISCUSSION

1. Ahab slandered Elijah as the "troubler" of Israel, when Ahab was in fact the problem. In what ways are the righteous slandered as "troublers" by society?

2. Obadiah was a man who served God faithfully in relative obscurity, and in the hostile environment of Ahab's house. How can Christians today follow Obadiah's example?

3. Some claim that religion (especially any religion that makes exclusive claims) has no place in the real world and should not be espoused publicly. What does the Bible say about this?

4. Have you ever relied upon the gods of materialism, government, relationships, health, pleasure, work, etc.? How so? Were you eventually disappointed? How so?

5. Read 1 Kings 18:21 and Joshua 24:15. How is choosing God vs. idols a *daily* choice?

9

ELIJAH VS. JEZEBEL

1 KINGS 19

Objective: To explore how and why
Elijah grew despondent in his ministry

INTRODUCTION

Among the most puzzling paradoxes of the spiritual life is that our greatest lows often follow on the heels of our greatest highs. In the immediate aftermath of his victory for the Lord at Carmel, Elijah fell off the cliff into a spiritual abyss and almost never recovered. The prophet had no desire to continue his ministry, but rather resigned himself to death. His Boss, however, refused his resignation. Only God's faithfulness kept Elijah from perishing in the abyss, proving that the Lord's most meaningful work is done when we are at our worst—not our best.

EXAMINATION

Read 1 Kings 19. Upon his return to his winter palace at Jezreel, Ahab informed his wife of what had happened at the contest on Carmel, and particularly of the massacre of Jezebel's prophets. Ahab had come dangerously close to giving all religious authority in Israel to Elijah and endorsing the national revival, so Jezebel had to act fast. In retaliation, she coldly and calculatingly sent a messenger to Elijah, swearing to dump his corpse in the waters of the Kishon (just like the other prophets) within 24 hours.

Elijah's response surprises us. From a man who had just faced down hundreds of prophets, summoned fire from heaven, and spurred a national revival, we would expect more courage and fortitude—and not a little swagger. But our gritty prophet is no more, transformed by fear into a coward. Like Obadiah, he knows the queen is capable of fulfilling her vow. At Jezebel's threat, Elijah fled for his life over a hundred miles south to Beersheba.

Leaving his servant at Beersheba, Elijah went another "day's journey" into the desert and collapsed under a broom or juniper tree. That Elijah went beyond Beersheba—the southern terminus of the Promised Land and as far from Jezebel as he could get without leaving Israel or Judah—alone into the wilderness may indicate that he was giving up on his ministry and mission completely. There under the tree, he begged God to take his life; it was only a matter of time before he died anyway.

While the prophet slept, a divine messenger appeared in answer to his prayer. Miraculously, there appeared beside Elijah a cake and some water. He was commanded to eat, and then he fell asleep again. Again, an angel appeared and woke him, ordering him to eat once more. Through this provision, God was preparing Elijah for a forty-day journey to a mountain that had not been a part of Israel's history since the time of Moses.

In a cave at Sinai, Elijah found shelter. It was then that he heard the Lord speak: "What are you doing here, Elijah?" God never asks a question to which he doesn't know the answer. Rather, he often asks such questions to beckon us out of self-deception and into self-disclosure (e.g., Gen. 3:9; 4:9). Elijah's reply was textbook narcissism, too often a byproduct of depression. The prophet professed his zeal for God and declared himself the lone righteous soul in Israel.

At this, God beckoned him to the opening of the cave, and as he had done with Moses, he now did with Elijah. The Lord's presence passed by Elijah at Sinai. The presence was followed by a great wind, an earthquake, and fire, but God was actually not present in any of these physical phenomena. The fire, however, was followed by a whisper, and it was in this gentle whisper that the Lord again asked, "What are you doing here, Elijah?"

Elijah's reply was the same as before, with only a very subtle shift in emphasis. To this, the Lord responded with a three-pronged commission:

anoint a new king over Aram, a new king over Israel, and a new prophet at Abel-meholah. In these three individuals, God would continue to accomplish his will for Israel and the world. He then concluded with a stark reminder to his despondent prophet: you aren't the only one living righteously. You are not alone (v. 18).

The Lord's command in v. 15, "Go, return on your way," was essentially a directive for Elijah to resume his prophetic ministry, the ministry the prophet had tried to abandon when he fled Beersheba for the wilderness. What is more, the divine instruction to anoint a Gentile named Hazael as king over Syria constituted a demonstration that God was sovereign, not just over Israel or Judah, but over all the nations of the world. Even today, there is not a ruler of men that does not answer to our cosmic King (Rev. 1:5).

In response to God's reassurances, Elijah made the journey to Abel-meholah to anoint Elisha. His choice of Elisha as his prophetic successor was expressed by casting his cloak on Elisha, a costly garment that clearly identified its bearer as holding the prophetic office. In so doing, he passed on to Elisha not only his mission, but also the divine ability to accomplish it. Before Elisha accepted the invitation to be Elijah's protégé and successor, he asked first to bid his family farewell, to which Elijah responded with something similar to "I have no problem with that," or, "Just remember you must follow me afterward." Elisha's selection was proof that God had not yet given up on Israel, and Elisha's final celebration with his family was evidence that he was making a clean break with his former life.

APPLICATION

Responding to Discouragement. In this story, Elijah made three crucial mistakes. First, he forgot to think theologically and, instead, merely reacted to circumstances. Thinking theologically would have helped him realize that the same God who had protected and provided for him then would do so now. Christians can weather terrible circumstances by recalling God's past faithfulness and provision. If Elijah had viewed his circumstances through the lens of God's previous acts, he might not have so easily succumbed to fear. Second, Elijah exposed an inordinate pride that had taken root in his heart as a result of his ministry successes (vv. 4, 10, 14). It's clear the prophet considered himself indispensable to what God was doing in Israel. Placed in such stark terms, such a mindset seems too absurd to be possible. But such thinking inevitably leads to depression, burnout, and collapse, and for the simple reason that we were never meant to carry the weight of the world successfully. We aren't wired that way. Pride gives way to stress, and stress gives way to falling off the cliff as Elijah did. Finally, Elijah stopped believing he was in a special relationship with God, and thus was "no better than my fathers" (v. 4). We serve a Commander-in-Chief who has never known defeat. Despite what we might think, setback is not a part of God's vocabulary. Paul claimed we are MORE than conquerors "through him who loved us" (Rom 8:37). It is God's favored election of his people that makes us victors. Elijah lost sight of this and panicked.

Do Your Job & Trust God. Elijah did not live to see the divine word fulfilled—but it was fulfilled. Upon his rapture to heaven, Elijah's ministry passed to Elisha, and the latter played a part in the accession of Hazael and Jehu over Syria and Israel, respectively. God's servants must remember that God's plan is to be fulfilled in his own time, that we must play our role as instructed. We must remember that, though we might live and die without seeing all that God will do, we can take our final breath confident that the Word of the Lord will surely come to pass (Matt. 24:35). In the meantime, we can rest assured that we serve a Lord who knows what it is like to be frustrated and weakened. Jesus was attended by angels in the desert (Matt. 4:1-11; cf. Luke 22:43), as was Elijah. And like the prophet, he left servants behind to continue the work. But he did not leave them as orphans. The Lord has never abandoned his people, and he never will. When we panic, feel defeated, and believe all is lost, let us do as Elijah did. Let us have a talk with the Lord. Let us recommit ourselves to his work and trust in his sovereignty. And let us leave the dark cave of self-pity behind for the fields ripe for harvest (1 Cor. 15:58).

No Reason to Fear. Too often, an older Christian will talk of how, in their opinion, the Lord's church is just one generation away from extinction. The implication seems to be that if the younger generation "mess this up," all that the Lord's church has accomplished since Acts 2 will be for not. Such egotistical hogwash is little better than Elijah moaning in the cave that he's the only righteous soul left, and what will be after him? Do not be deceived; God has always kept "seven thousand" in reserve who are faithful to him (cf. Isa. 10:20-23; 11:11-16; Amos 9:8). Jesus swore that the defenses of hell would never prevail against the church, that we would never be in retreat (Matt. 16:18). The church may grow unfaithful. She might dabble in apostasy. Her witness may go silent and her love grow cold—but the church shall never go extinct. Remember that the next time you grow fearful of what is to come. The future of Christ's bride is always bright, not because of your faithfulness or mine or that of our children, but because of her Husband. Even when we are faithless, he is faithful (2 Tim. 2:13). As long as there's a Christ, there will be a church of Christ.

CONCLUSION

With the close of 1 Kings 19, we will not hear much from Elijah until he is raptured to heaven. The bulk of his ministry is over. And though he cast a formidable shadow over Israel's history, such was due more to God's providence than Elijah's resilience. Even this strong prophet could be weak at times. Every Christian will feel weak at times, and those moments are reminders of our need to rely on the Lord all the more.

QUESTIONS FOR REFLECTION

1. Where did Elijah initially flee when Jezebel threatened him? What was the significance of this location?

2. Where did Elijah go at God's instruction? What was the significance of this location?

3. What various complaints did Elijah make to the Lord?

4. What three physical phenomena passed by the cave? Was God in any of them? What fourth phenomenon did God use to visit Elijah? What is the significance of this?

5. What "marching orders" did God give to Elijah?

6. To Elijah's objection that he was completely alone, what assurance did God give the prophet?

QUESTIONS FOR DISCUSSION

1. When threatened in the past, how have you failed to "think theologically"?

2. Have you allowed inordinate pride to take root in your heart in the past? Did it inevitably lead to discouragement? If so, how?

3. Why is it important to always remember our special relationship with God?

4. Even though we may not live to see God's word fulfilled, what hope do we have? How can this help us deal with discouragement?

5. Christ has sworn that his church will never suffer a setback or be defeated. How can this help us deal with discouragement?

6. How can older Christians be guilty of "generational arrogance"? How can older Christians inspire faith, positivity, and resilience in the next generation of Christians?

10

AHAB VS. ARAM

1 KINGS 20

Objective: To investigate Ahab's hostility to the word of God

INTRODUCTION

In the bio of Ahab in 1 Kings 16, there is a statement made in v. 34 that seems to have nothing to do with Ahab, but in fact has *everything* to do with him. Many years before, Joshua had cursed the city of Jericho (Josh. 6:34). Despite the curse, however, a man named Hiel decided to rebuild Jericho, and he lost his oldest and youngest sons as a result. This statement, though it concerns Hiel, tells us a lot about Ahab:

1.   Ahab is hostile to the word of God. It is believed that Hiel rebuilt Jericho at Ahab's command (Jewish tradition remembers Hiel as Ahab's top military commander). Ahab likely knew of the curse against the city, but scorned it.

2.   Ahab seeks to reverse the Conquest of Joshua. Instead of leaving pagan centers of power in ruins, he rebuilt them. This would not be the only way Ahab sought to bring Canaanite pagan practices back to the Promised Land.

3.   Ahab discovers that, despite his best efforts, the word of the Lord

stands forever (Isa. 55:11). A six-centuries-old curse on Jericho remained violently potent since it had originated from the mouth of the Lord. And if Hiel had spurned the divine warning and paid dearly for it, how much more so would Ahab, Jezebel, and all Israel suffer unless repentance and restoration were sought?

These three facts about Ahab from 1 Kings 16:34 will serve as a lens as we study 1 Kings 20-22. In 1 Kings 20, we learn how Ahab was hostile to the word of God.

EXAMINATION

Read 1 Kings 20:1-25. Early in Ahab's reign, the nation of Syria felt pressure to their north from the Assyrian empire. Aram's trade routes to the north had been severed by Assyria, and when Omri of Israel conquered Moab, Syria lost access to the King's Highway trade route in Transjordan. Also, Ahab and Jezebel's marriage had jeopardized Aram's alliance with the Phoenicians. But if Ben-hadad, Aram's king, could subdue Israel, he would regain access to trade via Mediterranean ports and Phoenician trading vessels in Tyre. Moreover, the king of Syria also knew that Israel was coming off a three-year famine; Samaria surely could not endure a lengthy siege. What did Syria have to lose?

Ben-hadad smugly sent a demand to Ahab using language very common for its day (v. 3). Though the demands were humiliating to Ahab, Israel's king gladly and quickly capitulated. But then Ben-hadad altered the terms, making them even more humiliating and unreasonable. This Ahab rejected (rather than just being greedy, Ben-hadad might have been intentionally picking a fight). When Ahab put the matter to the elders of the people, they too thought Ben-hadad's demands unreasonable.

At this point, an unnamed prophet appears with a message from the Lord, and it was intended primarily for Ahab (the second person pronouns in v. 13 are singular). "You see that massive army that stands against you? I'm going to defeat it today on your behalf so that you know I'm real and that I'm your God." The Lord instructed Ahab first to send out 232 "servants of the governors of the districts," which is a complicated phrase. The Hebrew means "servant" or "child" and can refer to trained military personnel. But Provan points out that the term "elsewhere in Kings never requires such a military sense" (cf. 3:7; 11:17, 28; 14:3, 17; 18:43; 19:3). In fact, the same term is used of David in 1 Samuel 17:33. There, as here, God was using his "foolishness" to shame the world's military "wisdom" and prove the battle always belongs to him.

What we are left with is an impressive scene. While Ben-hadad enjoyed a kegger in his tent with his allies and officers, 232 young Israelite servants—wielding all the military shock and awe of a Cub Scout troop—threw the Syrian camp into a tizzy. The 7,000 that made up Israel's army (v. 14) were sent out to mop up the carnage, and Ben-hadad was forced to beat a path back to Damascus on horseback with his tail between his legs.

At the end of the battle, the nameless prophet reappeared with a warning for Ahab: Don't get too comfortable because Ben-hadad would return in the Spring with a vengeance. Meanwhile, Ben-hadad's advisors blamed the defeat on the fact that Israel's god held a military advantage in the hill country; on the plains, however, Aram's gods would prove superior. But such ignorance only blinded Syria to the truth, and just as Elijah's victory at Carmel proved God's superiority over Baal, the next battle would demonstrate his sovereignty over Aram's pantheon.

The king's advisors also counseled him to relieve his 32 allies of command over their own troops and replace them with Aram's own commanders, streamlining the chain-of-command and giving everyone a common objective. Perhaps in their panic—so the reasoning went—the allied chiefs had abandoned their allegiance to Ben-hadad, failed to act in concert with one another, and adopted an "every man for himself" mentality. Ironically, however, and as we will soon learn, both Ben-hadad and Ahab missed the day's real lesson: Military size matters not at all if the Lord is for/against you (Prov. 21:31).

Read 1 Kings 20:26-43. Sure enough, Ben-hadad invaded Israel again in the Spring and met them at Aphek. The Syrians had been successful in mustering another large army; Israel's force, meanwhile, is described by the narrator as "two little flocks of goats" (v. 27). But those for whom the Lord fights are never outnumbered or like lambs led to the slaughter. The anonymous prophet again informed Ahab that God would fight for his people, this time to teach the Syrians a lesson. Syria falsely presumed that the Lord was limited to the hills, and the God of Israel is always interested in setting the record straight when it comes to his consistent character and transcendent glory. God would again deliver Israel so that they would know he was the Lord.

After a week of military stand-still (a period of time perhaps intended to remind us of Jericho), the two sides went at it. Israel defeated 100,000 and sent the rest fleeing for the safety of Aphek's fortified walls. But in another event deliberately reminiscent of Jericho, the city wall collapsed, claiming another 27,000 casualties. Meanwhile, a panicked Ben-hadad holed up in an "undisclosed location" in the heart of the city. His aides reminded him that the kings of Israel were known to be trustworthy (the text literally says, "kings of loyalty"), and that if Ben-adad played the part of a prisoner-slave eager to do Ahab's bidding, he might escape with his life. Thus, Ben-hadad and his entourage paraded before the Israelites in sackcloth and with nooses around their necks (the ancient equivalent of putting on an orange jumpsuit and handcuffing yourself), playing the part of captured slaves, expressing their willingness to submit and serve. Sure enough, Ahab fell for the ruse, inviting the Syrian into his royal chariot to parlay as a "brother" (v. 32). In their negotiation, Ben-hadad promised to restore the cities Syria had seized from Israel, as well as give Israelite merchants access to the markets in Damascus, and Ahab agreed.

At this point, one would think the story would be over. However, as Richard Nelson puts it, "Biblical narrative sometimes sneaks up on the reader to deliver an unexpected blow." And this is indeed where the story takes a strange turn. At the instigation of God, a prophet (the same as vv. 13, 22, 28?) told his fellow prophet to strike him, but the fellow prophet refused. For his disobedience, it was prophesied that the fellow prophet would be mauled by a lion (cf. 13:24), and that's exactly what happened. The first prophet then found someone else to strike him, and it left a wound near his eyes which allowed him to don a bandage as if he were a wounded soldier.

As he approached Ahab, the disguised prophet "confessed" to allowing a POW to escape, and the penalty would be either the "soldier's" life or a fine of a talent of silver (cf. Exod. 22:7-13), and since he could never pay such an exorbitant sum (cf. Matt. 18:23-24), his penalty would be death (cf. Acts 16:27). Ahab responded with something akin to, "Yep, those are the options for your punishment. You choose." At that point, the "soldier" removed his disguise, and Ahab instantly recognized him as one of the prophets. Ahab was then chastised for showing clemency to someone whom God had "devoted to destruction" (v. 42), and just as Ahab was so willing for the soldier to lose his life for allowing his prisoner to escape, so God would exact Ahab's life as a penalty for letting Ben-hadad off the hook.

Modern readers of this story will likely wonder why it was such a big deal for Ahab to show clemency toward Ben-hadad instead of executing him. However, whenever Israel went out to battle at the Lord's command, they were expected to operate under the rules of holy war, of which the end result was that everything placed under God's ban must die. How was Ahab expected to know that his struggle with Ben-hadad was holy war? Consider that:

- Ben-hadad intended to reduce Samaria to rubble; for Israel, threat of utter destruction must be met with utter destruction.

- The battle of Aphek was essentially a reenactment of Jericho—seven days and the walls fall down.

- God had given Ahab the battle strategy as he often did with Moses, Joshua, Gideon, etc.

But the ultimate reason Ahab should have known better is that the anonymous prophet had made clear God would give Israel victory so that Ahab would know that the Lord was God—not Baal. In other words, God was acting to glorify himself and make himself known to Ahab. Ahab, however, used his God-given victory as an opportunity to gratify himself and achieve his own purposes. As he had proven with his order to resurrect Jericho, Ahab had nothing but scorn for God's word, which amounts to scorn for God's name—a name he jealously protects.

APPLICATION

God of the Hills. The statement in v. 23 on the lips of the Syrians seems primitive. But we, too, can be tempted to think that God is potent in some areas of life, while ineffective or uninterested in others. Though such a confession might never make it to our lips, we might subscribe to a more subtle form of this pagan theology, as Benjamin Franklin did. He once wrote the preacher George Whitefield, "I rather suspect, from certain circumstances, that though the general government of the universe is well administered, our particular little affairs are perhaps below notice, and left to take the chance of human prudence or imprudence, as either may happen to be uppermost." The reality, however, is there is not a molecule, atom, or speck of dust in the universe that is beyond God's concern or control. If he notices when birds fall from the sky and has numbered the hairs on our heads (Matt 10:29-31), we can be sure God reigns in merciful majesty over both the hills and the plains.

Faithful Stewards. It would be absurd to suggest that the point of this story is that we should wipe out all the enemies of God on earth. Rather, a more universal truth can be found in the fact that Ahab was not a faithful steward of what God put in his hands. Ahab received divine deliverance and the call to prosecute holy war against Ben-hadad. God even gave the enemy king into Ahab's hands, and relief from all future oppression by Ben-hadad would be mitigated. But Ahab scorned God's word and sought to manipulate circumstances for his own benefit. Christians today must respect God's gifts and use them to bless the lives of others and ultimately to the glory of God, rather than manipulate those same gifts for personal gain.

Unmerited Favor. It is an understatement to say Ahab and Samaria did not deserve deliverance from the Syrian threat. But God did so out of grace and in order to make himself known to his people, primarily Ahab. In the same way, when we receive unmerited favor from God, the proper response is to acknowledge him as Lord and God and give him our faith and obedience. Any other response is a foolish rejection of something we didn't deserve in the first place.

CONCLUSION

When Ahab gave the command to rebuild Jericho, he demonstrated a hostility towards the word of God. When he granted leniency to Ben-hadad, a person God had devoted to destruction, Ahab did it again. No one is immune from showing hostility towards God's word, not even Christians. It starts when we fail to take God seriously, when we think we know better than God, or we simply don't care about the consequences until it's too late.

QUESTIONS FOR REFLECTION

1. Why did Ben-hadad reject Ahab's initial offer of surrender?

2. According to v. 13, what reason did God have for delivering Israel and Ahab?

3. Who were the "servants of the governors of the districts"? Why were they significant to the story?

4. What reason did Syria give for their defeat in the first battle?

5. What details of the second battle remind you of the battle of Jericho?

6. Why did God send a prophet to denounce Ahab's leniency toward Ben-hadad?

7. How was Ahab supposed to know that he was engaged in holy war?

QUESTIONS FOR DISCUSSION

1. Re-read Benjamin Franklin's statement to George Whitefield in the Application section. What examples of this mindset have you observed?

2. Why is it important to believe God is interested in and sovereign over all aspects of life?

3. Like Ahab, how can people, even Christians, show hostility to the word of God in their lives?

4. Have you ever witnessed someone manipulate God's blessing for personal gain? How so?

5. Have you been faithful in taking God's unmerited favor towards you and using it for his glory? If so, how? If not, what do you need to do different?

11

AHAB VS. NABOTH

1 KINGS 21

Objective: To explore competing views of power
and how God holds tyrants accountable

INTRODUCTION

Naboth's story is a pivotal moment in 1-2 Kings. Whereas the narrator previously had been satisfied to mention and dismiss kings with a few short
verses, he has slowed the pace of storytelling considerably when it comes to
Ahab. As Ahab's power grows, the reader is left to wonder if this king will
ever be punished for his unprecedented evil.

Just when we start to think God has grown impotent or indifferent
regarding Israel's sin, or that Elijah has succumbed to the futility of his calling, the re-energized prophet crashes onto the scene with a judgment from
heaven. Might doesn't make right. As long as God—not Baal—is Lord of
heaven, unprecedented evil will always meet an abhorrent end.

EXAMINATION

Read 1 Kings 21. The story takes place in Jezreel, where Naboth owned a
vineyard. Jezreel served as Ahab's winter retreat (18:46), being at a lower el-

evation than Samaria. The double mention of Jezreel in v. 1 reinforces that this place was Naboth's ancestral hometown, which is a crucial detail in the narrative, as is the fact that he seems to be a part of the local aristocracy (v. 12). Naboth's refusal to sell his land is rooted in more than a "Daddy won't sell the farm" sentimentality. The word translated "forbid" (v. 3) indicates that the sale would have been a profane thing in God's eyes, a desecration of a divine gift.

Land was a big deal in ancient Israel. It had been promised to Abraham and his descendants in perpetuity (Gen. 17:8), but only as tenants; God was still the landowner (Lev. 25:23). The tribes of Israel had received their various inheritances from the Lord once Joshua's campaigns were completed (Josh. 13:1-7); they were stewards of what God had given them. In his book, *God's People in God's Land*, Christopher Wright makes this very intriguing observation:

> Although admittedly an argument from silence, it is nevertheless an impressive fact that the whole Old Testament provides not a single case of an Israelite voluntarily selling land outside his family group [...] This silence of the text is matched by the absence as yet of any inscriptional evidence from Palestine of Israelite sale and purchase of land, though there is abundant evidence of such transactions from Canaanite and surrounding societies.

The very fact, then, that Ahab made an offer for Naboth's vineyard demonstrates what little regard the king had for God's Law. What's worse, Ahab had plans to turn this beautiful vineyard—something that took time and diligence to cultivate properly—into a common vegetable garden. It would be like plowing up beautiful rose bushes to make way for kale. The only other place in the Old Testament that uses the phrase "vegetable garden" is Deuteronomy 11:10 in a reference to Egypt. Ahab, in a way, wants to take Israel back to Egypt. More accurately, he wants to re-Canaanize the Promised Land.

His offer to Naboth rebuffed, Ahab did what all great and powerful kings do when they don't get what they want—he went to his bedroom and pouted. Jezebel's response is chilling—her rhetorical question in v. 7 contains an emphasis on "you" and "I" in the Hebrew text: i.e. "Is this how you act as king over Israel? Get up and eat! Cheer up. I'll get you the vineyard of Naboth the Jezreelite." Behind Jezebel's scornful question of her husband lay a wholly different view (a Canaanite one) of power and property than the one God inscribed within the Torah (cf. Deut. 17:14-20; 1 Sam. 8:11-18). In regards to property, the Law made clear that the Lord owned the land, and Israel was his tenant. Israel's pagan neighbors, however, believed that all property was owned by the crown, with the citizens living on it as tenants—all land was on grant from the king.

The queen got to work mailing letters with instructions to bring trumped-up charges of blasphemy and treason against Naboth, a crime which carried the death penalty (Exod. 22:27). Everything was to be done according to the letter of the Law. Amazing that the one time Jezebel (or Ahab) showed any concern for Israel's Law, they do so for their own selfish gain. A kangaroo court was called into session, Naboth was found guilty of blasphemy, and the righteous landowner was stoned to death. With that, Jezebel informed an elated Ahab that the vineyard was now his to enjoy, and the crown quickly confiscated the owner-less land.

But this travesty of justice triggered another showdown between king and prophet. Note that God told Elijah exactly where he could find the king—despite the immoral power play, the narrator still calls it the "vineyard of Naboth" (v. 18). Walter Brueggemann is right when he observes, "Royal manipulation does not alter the true identity of the land!" Ahab had gained the land, but God remembered who was the rightful owner.

Elijah bore a message that Ahab's blood would be lapped up by the same dogs that had lapped Naboth's; in fact, all of Ahab's family was destined for the dogs (2 Kgs. 9:25-26, 36-37; 10:10-11, 17). Arguably, no greater disgrace in death existed in the mind of an ancient Israelite; in ancient times, dogs did not enjoy the "man's best friend" status they do today. Rather, they were considered "unclean scavengers worthy of scorn." A contemporary Assyrian curse declared "let dogs tear his unburied body to pieces." In Homer's *Iliad*, as Achilles stands over the dying Hector, he boasts, "You the dogs and birds will rip apart shamefully … the dogs and birds will devour you wholly."

Ahab's response was a hostile one—"My enemy! So, you've run me down!" (v. 20 Msg). Perhaps Elijah had been absent for so long that Ahab had thought the prophet had met his demise. But the prophet's arrival impressed on Ahab that he couldn't escape judgment. The king could pitch a fit and have his rival executed in order to seize a coveted vineyard, but he remained subject to the divine Landlord. Because the king had provoked the wrath of God in such an unprecedented way, Ahab's entire line would be eliminated (v. 21). From the world's perspective, Naboth was a nobody. But in the Lord's eyes, he was a righteous member of the covenant community and a bearer of God's image, so his illegal execution triggered the collapse of a dynasty.

But then the twist comes. Just when we feel led to believe that Ahab has no conscience, no soul, no remorse—he repents! He engaged in all the typical ancient practices associated with grief and remorse (Num. 14:6; Josh. 7:6; Judg. 11:35; 2 Sam. 1:2; 3:31). God saw his heart and had mercy; he informed Ahab through the prophet that he would delay Ahab's judgment, just as he would later do for Nineveh (Jon. 3:10) and Hezekiah (2 Kgs. 20:1, 6, 11). Due to God's grace, Ahab would live another few years, and his sons about fourteen after that. Even an unprecedented degenerate—when he repents—can receive mercy, for God desires that no one perish in his wrath (Ezek. 18:32; 2 Pet. 3:9).

APPLICATION

The Wrath of God. God uses strong language in his denunciation of Ahab (cf. vv. 19, 21, 23-24). Lest we deem God to be too vengeful for doling out a $50,000 punishment for a 50¢ crime, the narrator reminds us that Ahab and Jezebel had been unprecedented in their evil. Not since the previous inhabitants of the Promised Land had there been such evil in this land (vv. 25-26). Just as God had done with the Amorites, he would now, in his righteousness, vomit out of the land a wicked king and queen for trying to procure land illicitly. Such wrath points forward to the day when Jesus, in flaming fire, will take vengeance on the disobedient (2 Thess. 1:8), a promise Paul made to those who were oppressed. When God's people suffer, instead of seeking vengeance for ourselves, we must leave room for God's wrath (Rom. 12:19).

Hierarchy of Power. In ancient Israel, God was Israel's king, and the mortal king on Israel's throne was merely his agent to lend a hand to the downtrodden and administer justice. In short, the king of Israel didn't sit atop the totem pole, and he certainly was not above the law, but was first among equals. On the other hand, as a pagan, Jezebel would have subscribed to the golden rule—he who has the gold, makes the rules. Might makes right. Note that Ahab pouted at first because he saw no other way to get the vineyard. But Jezebel had no scruples with killing Naboth if it meant getting what she and Ahab wanted. God desires that rulers serve those entrusted to their care, rather than seeing the governed as existing for the prestige and pleasure of the ruler. When rulers (in families, in churches, in businesses, in government) bully those under them for personal gain, God takes notice, and will pour out his wrath in due time. God's leaders must always seek to be a channel of his blessing to those they rule/serve.

CONCLUSION

Too often, we are reminded of how easy it is in life to abuse power and mistreat the weak. Hatred, greed, and lust for power can seem to be invincible forces. But reigning over all the powers and forces of the world is a holy, supreme God who has sworn to champion the cause of the powerless and punish the strong in his wrath. When it seems like might makes right, Christians can trust that God will one day right every wrong. In the meantime, we must ascribe to the New Testament's ultimate Golden Rule: treat others as God has treated us in Christ (cf. Eph. 4:32).

QUESTIONS FOR REFLECTION

1. Why is Jezreel mentioned so often in the opening verses of 1 Kings 21?

2. Why did Naboth refuse to sell the land to Ahab?

3. How did Israel view land and power differently than their pagan neighbors?

4. In what way was Jezebel careful to obey the Law of Moses in this story? How is this ironic?

5. Even after Naboth's death, why did God still refer to it as "the vineyard of Naboth"?

6. What sentence did God lay on Ahab for his crime? What was Ahab's response?

QUESTIONS FOR DISCUSSION

1. What examples of "might makes right" have you witnessed in the world?

2. Why should we be wary when evil people are suddenly concerned about "following the rules"?

3. What does God's punishment of Ahab tell us about God's wrath?

4. What hope do Christians have when the weak are trampled by the strong?

5. How does Jesus' exercise of power in John 13 contrast with Ahab's?

6. How can Christian leaders be better about leveraging their power and influence?

12

AHAB VS. GOD

1 KINGS 22

Objective: To affirm that God's Word always comes to pass, but we can become incapable of believing it by being hard-hearted

INTRODUCTION

It seems Ahab's wickedness knows no bounds, and though he seemed sincere, we are left to wonder if Ahab's repentance at the end of 1 Kings 21 will last. Sure enough, Ahab began to spurn the word of the Lord once again, and God decided that he must be eliminated. Ahab subsequently attempted to outthink God, but failed. This arrogant king learned the hard way that, try as he might, the word of the Lord will come to pass.

EXAMINATION

Read 1 Kings 22:1-40. The treaty struck in 1 Kings 20 had survived for about three years. But the city of Ramoth-gilead was never returned to Ahab and Israel. Ahab wanted to rush into things, but Jehoshaphat wisely insisted on inquiring of the Lord before going into battle. At his request, Ahab summoned four hundred prophets to tip him off as to the battle's outcome. Their take? The Lord had already given Ramoth-gilead into Ahab's hands.

But the prophets' positive report seemed a little bit too convenient for Jehoshaphat's conscience and he asked for a prophet of the Lord to be summoned (v. 7). Ahab objected to such a notion, but sent for one anyway. While Micaiah was being summoned, a prophet named Zedekiah seized the spotlight by theatrically demonstrating the beatdown Ahab was sure to give the Syrians. In this case, iron horns represented brute power and overwhelming military might. All signs seemed to be pointing to a smashing victory for Ahab and Jehoshaphat.

The messenger sent to fetch Micaiah didn't hesitate to remind the prophet what was expected of him (v. 13). Everyone else had spoken a favorable word, and Micaiah had better fall in line if he knew what was good for him. But Micaiah's response is a bold example of the resiliency required of every man and woman of God (v. 14).

When prompted by Ahab to say whether Ramoth-gilead should be attacked, Micaiah surprises us by affirming what the other 400 prophets had said. Yes! God had given the city into Ahab's hands already. It was as good as his. But then the story takes a weird turn. We would expect someone like Ahab to grin from ear to ear, call for his armor, and ride off into dubious battle. But he doesn't. He instead cried, "Baloney!" on what Micaiah had spoken (v. 16).

The prophet responded with the truth—Israel would be scattered like sheep without a shepherd, a common metaphor indicating the death of a king. Without a king to lead, a nation would be destroyed by division and ruin. Implicit in Micaiah's words may be a judgment on Ahab that he had not been the shepherd to his people he should have been.

And then Micaiah dramatically pulled back the cosmic curtain to give Ahab (and us) a glimpse at what had really happened behind the scenes. The prophet claimed to have stood in the midst of the divine council in heaven, before God on his throne. The Lord asked his council how Ahab might be enticed to attack Ramoth-gilead; in the midst of the debate, "a spirit came forward and stood before the LORD," offering to deceive the king through his prophets. This proposal met with the Lord's approval (vv. 21-22).

It is a disturbing idea that God deceives Ahab, so note that it is a deceiving spirit that goes out to manipulate the king through his prophets—God himself is not deceiving anyone. This dynamic is exactly what Paul discussed in his second letter to the Thessalonians (2 Thess. 2:11-12). If we love God and seek him, we need not worry that he will deceive us (Psa. 18:25-26).

To put it more plainly, though God cannot lie, he is not above "pushing our buttons" in order to accomplish his will. Though it is possible to act against God's ideal or circumstantial will, no one can thwart his ultimate will. Part of what makes God gloriously omnipotent is that he is able and willing to use human selfishness and sin to accomplish his good pleasure. Just as he hardened Pharaoh's heart—and allowed Pharaoh to harden his own heart—in order to glorify himself and accomplish his will (cf. Exod. 7:3-5, 13-14, 22; 8:15, 19; 9:12; 14:1-14), so God used Ahab's petulant self-will to trigger the king's own "disaster" (v. 23; cf. Prov. 21:1).

Though he brought a false message, Micaiah also brought a true message, and the irony is that both came directly from God. In other words, the Lord is above reproach since he tells Ahab, "I allowed these prophets to lie to you in order to trigger your destruction. Now that you know what will happen, choose for yourself whether you love me and the truth vs. your petulant self-will and self-delusion."

When the Israel/Judah coalition met Ben-hadad's army at Ramoth-gilead, Ahab encouraged Jehoshaphat to enter the fray in his royal robes, while Ahab himself went incognito, surely guaranteeing that Judah's king—not Israel's—would be the easier target. And just as Ahab arguably hoped, the Syrians gave chase to Jehoshaphat, but only because they mistook him somehow for Ahab.

"But a certain man drew his bow at random and struck the king of Israel between the scale armor and the breastplate" (v. 34). In this singular statement are no less than three supposed "coincidences" the narrator invites us to contemplate.

- It was "a certain man," known only to the Most High God, who drew in his bow the fatal arrow that delivered ultimate disaster to Ahab. In other words, this was not an elite warrior.

- This archer "drew his bow at random." He did not aim specifically at Ahab. In other words, what appeared to have been dumb luck was a carefully orchestrated act of the divine will.

- The arrow found its place "between the scale armor and the breastplate." Ancient body armor had interconnected scales and plates; not many gaps would have existed in this armor, and those that did would have been small. Yet this arrow "just happened" to strike Ahab in one of the very few places where he was most vulnerable.

Knowing he had been mortally wounded, Ahab commanded his driver to wheel around and carry him behind the lines, from whence he watched the remainder of the battle. As the day turned to night, Ahab bled out in his chariot, and Israel's army dispersed to a thousand hills like sheep without a shepherd (v. 36)—just as God had said. Ahab was buried in Samaria; his chariot was washed in the pool of Samaria, allowing dogs and local whores to frolic in his blood—just as God had said.

Read 1 Kings 22:41-50. Like his father, Asa, Jehoshaphat was a righteous king, but failed to exterminate the scourge of idolatry in Judah completely (v. 43). In addition to tolerating idolatry to some degree, Jehoshaphat had a cozy relationship with Ahab and Jezebel—his son married their daughter (2 Kgs. 8:18). One thing in his favor is that he wiped out the practice of prostitution at the cult shrines and high places (cf. 15:12; Deut. 23:17-18).

The narrator of Kings also tells us that Jehoshaphat held influence over Edom, just as Solomon had. But he didn't have Solomon's luck (9:26-28) when it came to maritime trade. When Jehoshaphat's ships were destroyed while in port at Ezion-geber (on the Gulf of Aqaba), Ahab's son proposed a joint venture, something to which Jehoshaphat did not agree. Through the prophet Eliezer, Chronicles explains that the ships' destruction was because Jehoshaphat had built them in collaboration with Ahaziah (2 Chron. 20:35-37). Duly warned, Judah's righteous king knew better than to attempt such folly a second time.

APPLICATION

Yes Men. Ahab unwisely surrounded himself with sycophantic prophets who clearly were determined to tell him what they thought he already wanted to hear. This in part led to Ahab's demise, a reminder that unanimous agreement may not be as great as we think, and disagreement may not be as unhealthy as we believe. Being ornery or disagreeable is never acceptable. But healthy churches need not be intimidated by dissent, especially when it might be that some are blind and deaf, with eyes only for their own ambitions and ears only for what they want to hear. Let us always put a premium on those who speak truth in the name of the Lord, regardless of what it does to their popularity or personal safety.

Doomed to Doubt. This final episode of Ahab's life is a cautionary tale regarding the consequences of unbelief and scorn for the Word of God. He became so antagonistic to the truth and wallowed so deeply in self-delusion that he became incapable of believing God's word, even when it was spoken for Ahab's good—perhaps especially when it was spoken for his good. People can become so hostile to God's Word that they cannot believe his Word when spoken for their good. They have no love for the truth, and so God hands them over to be deceived and deluded again and again (cf. Rom. 1:24-28). Even in their delusion, however, God sends messengers into their life to shake them back to reality, and though a part of them knows the warning to be valid, they fail to act so as to prevent disaster. It happened to Ahab; it can happen to us; it can happen to anyone.

Spiritual Disguises. Rather than trust and obey, some are like Ahab and adopt disguises in a dubious attempt to circumvent God. As objective observers, we recognize Ahab's disguise was an exercise in futility, but our attempts at camouflage are just as futile and foolish. "Adultery" and "homosexuality" are now an "affair" and "alternate lifestyle." "Sin" has been reconceptualized as a "mistake." Fundamentally bad, Scripture-denigrating decisions are said to be "Spirit-led" and an opportunity to "step out in faith." A prerequisite for any right relationship with God is shedding our "disguises," owning up to and being open about our sins, and allowing the sunlight of truth to sanitize our corrupted hearts. Where there is equivocation over sin and fraternity with falsehood, deception, and disguises, there can be no fellowship with He who has 20/20 vision.

CONCLUSION

The tragedy of Ahab's life and death is made more depressing by the realization that he was a capable king in so many other ways. Despite a three-year drought and defeat by the Syrians (both triggered by Ahab's apostasy), Israel was mostly secure during his reign. Here at the end, the narrator reminds us of Ahab's many building projects (v. 39). But all the wealth and opulence and administrative acuity and military success in the world are worthless if one does not trust the Word of the Lord and obey it.

QUESTIONS FOR REFLECTION

1. Though 400 prophets predicted victory, why did Jehoshaphat insist on consulting a prophet of the Lord?

2. When commanded by the messenger to tell Ahab what he wanted to hear, how did Micaiah respond?

3. What heavenly vision did Micaiah relate to Ahab?

4. Though God sent forth a deceiving spirit, is God guilty of lying in this story? Explain your answer.

5. What did Ahab do in battle in an attempt to circumvent God's plan?

6. What three supposed "coincidences" does the narrator note in relating Ahab's death?

QUESTIONS FOR DISCUSSION

1. Have you ever been part of a group where disagreement and dissent were frowned upon? Did you see such an attitude lead to dysfunction? How so?

2. How can Christians discern between a disagreeable person and a person speaking a word of truth and warning to the deceived?

3. Read 2 Thess. 2:9-12. What does it look like in real life to "love the truth."

4. Have you known someone who, through rebellion and hostility, became incapable of believing God? Did you witness God trying to reach that person, even in their delusion?

5. In what ways have you attempted to disguise yourself before God? Were you successful? What happened?

6. How does God go about stripping us of our "disguises"?